Vintage Knit Knacks

Sue Culligan

Running Press
Philadelphia · London

Contents

Vintage
Knit Knacks

Sue Culligan

First published in the United States in 2011 by Running Press Book Publishers
A Member of the Perseus Books Group

Books published by Running Press are available at special discounts for bulk purchases in the United States by corporations, institutions, and other organizations. For more information, please contact the Special Markets Department at the Perseus Books Group, 2300 Chestnut Street, Suite 200, Philadelphia, PA 19103, or call (800) 810-4145, ext. 5000, or e-mail special.markets@perseusbooks.com.

ISBN 978-0-7624-4341-3
Library of Congress Control Number: 2011934433

9   8   7   6   5   4   3   2   1
Digit on the right indicates the number of this printing

Conceived, designed, and produced by
Quid Publishing
Level 4, Sheridan House
114 Western Road
Hove BN3 1DD
England

Photography by Andrew Perris
Cover and interior design: Rawshock Design

Running Press Book Publishers
2300 Chestnut Street
Philadelphia, PA 19103-4371

Visit us on the web!
www.runningpress.com

Introduction

VINTAGE KNIT KNACKS IS A HOMEY COLLECTION OF DESIGNS inspired by past and present trends. The 20 projects are classic designs with a twist, and include a mix of decorative, useful, and wearable items. These range from a sophisticated wall clock (see page 134) and a colorful plant-pot cover (see page 100), through to an elegant pair of fingerless lace gloves (see page 126).

In keeping with the vintage theme, the yarns used for the projects are mainly pure wool or cotton, with the occasional hint of silk and alpaca blends for added luxury. The result is a collection of highly tactile shapes in gorgeous natural fibers. The color palette ranges from soft neutral shades in cream and gray, through faded retro colors in green, terra-cotta, and duck-egg blue, to rich earthy shades of rust and peat. You can, of course, change the shades in any of the projects to suit the color scheme in your own home. And to complete the vintage look, search out antique buttons to use as fasteners and colorful floral fabrics for backings and linings.

Beautiful photography shows each project clearly in simple surroundings, with close-up shots emphasizing stitch detail and other decorative embellishments. Step-by-step instructions guide you through each stage of the pattern, and charts have been included where required. Tip boxes offer useful hints and suggestions for customizing the projects, covering everything from alternative colorways and embellishments to changing the sizes of some of the designs.

The projects are listed in order of skill level, starting with the most basic and progressing through to the more challenging patterns. Most are easy to make and provide a good introduction to different methods and stitches. If you are relatively new to knitting, the "Basics" section (see page 8) will guide you through various ways of casting on and binding off and the stitches used throughout the book, as well as giving some tips for finishing off a project.

1

The Basics

The projects in this book incorporate lots of techniques—including lace, fair isle, cabling, and beading—and range in complexity from simple to more challenging. As a result, this is a perfect collection of designs for novice knitters, for whom the following pages provide an introduction to the basic equipment and techniques required. Experienced knitters may prefer to skip to the projects themselves (see page 18).

Materials and Equipment

KNITTING YARN

Yarn is available in various fibers, either natural—such as wool, alpaca, angora, cashmere, cotton, silk, and linen—or from manmade fibers like acrylic and nylon. Some yarns will be a blend of different fibers.

Yarn also comes in different thicknesses, starting with very fine laceweight yarns and 2-ply through to 3-ply, 4-ply, double-knit, aran, chunky, and superchunky. It is sold with an accompanying label or ball band that states the yardage, gauge, shade name or number, and dye lot. It is important to use the same dye lot if you are knitting a project in one color, as the color can vary between different batches.

The yarns used for the projects in this book are mainly natural fibers and can all be sourced online. Alternatively, they can be replaced with different yarns of your choice—just remember to check that the gauge, needle size, and yardage are similar. The gauge can be adjusted slightly by increasing or decreasing the size of needle used. Always knit a gauge square before starting a project and check it against the suggested gauge.

KNITTING NEEDLES

Knitting needles come in a range of sizes, lengths, and materials (most commonly aluminum, plastic, wood, or bamboo).

Straight knitting needles, sold in pairs, are the most commonly used in knitting patterns and are suitable for most standard projects.

Circular needles are comprised of two knitting needle tips joined by a flexible cord. These are used for knitting in the round or for knitting large or heavy projects.

Double-pointed needles are sold in sets of four or five. They are usually shorter than standard straight needles and have a pointed tip at each end. These are used for knitting in the round, most commonly for small projects such as socks, hats, and gloves. Double-pointed needles are also necessary for knitting i-cord (see page 16).

CROCHET HOOKS

Crochet hooks are available in a similar range of sizes to knitting needles. Some of the knitted projects in this book require basic crochet edging or a crochet loop.

This cell phone cover is fastened with a basic crochet loop (see pages 60-63).

ACCESSORIES

There are many knitting accessories available, but these are some of the most useful.

Knitting needle gauge: this will tell you the size of your knitting needle; it is particularly helpful for sizing double-pointed needles and circular needles, which often don't have the size stamped on them.

Row counter: a small plastic tally that can be changed at the end of each row; important for working complicated cable or lace patterns and when working from a chart.

Cable needle: a short double-pointed needle that is used for working cable patterns.

Stitch holder: a large safety pin for holding stitches that you need to go back to work on later.

Tapestry needle: a sewing needle with a blunt end and large eye for threading yarn through.

Stitch markers: small rings that can be slipped onto a needle to mark a certain stitch or to mark the end of the round on circular knitting.

Techniques

Casting On

There are various methods of casting on. The most commonly used are the thumb and cable methods, but you can choose whichever you find easiest.

Thumb Method

1. Holding the needle in your right hand, measure out a tail of yarn roughly three times the length of the edge to be cast on. Make a slip knot and place it on the needle.

2. Wrap the tail end over your thumb, place the tip of the needle under the yarn at the front of your thumb, and knit a stitch by passing the ball end of the yarn over the needle.

3. Continue until the required number of stitches are on the needle.

Cable Method

1. Make a slip knot and place it on the left-hand needle.

2. Insert the right-hand needle in the slip knot, pass the yarn around the needle as if you are going to knit a stitch, draw the loop through, and place on the left-hand needle.

3. Place the right-hand needle between the two stitches on the left-hand needle, pass the yarn around the right-hand needle as if you are going to knit a stitch, draw the loop through, and place on the left-hand needle.

4. Place the right-hand needle between the two stitches nearest the tip of the left-hand needle, pass the yarn around the right-hand needle, and draw the loop through as before.

5. Continue until the required number of stitches are on the left-hand needle.

French Cast-On

1. Make a slip knot and place it on the left-hand needle.

2. Insert the right-hand needle in the slip knot, pass the yarn around the needle as if you are going to knit a stitch, draw the loop through, and place on the left-hand needle.

3. Place the right-hand needle in the stitch just made, pass the yarn around the needle, and draw the loop through as before.

4. Continue until the required number of stitches are on the left-hand needle.

Long-Tail Cast-On

1. Work as stage 1 of thumb method.

2. Wrap the tail end of the yarn over your thumb and the ball end of the yarn around the index finger. Place the tip of the needle under the yarn at the front of your thumb and knit a stitch by passing the ball end of the yarn over the needle.

3. Release the thumb loop and pull it tight around the needle, keeping the ball end around the index finger.

Binding Off

This is the term used for finishing off your piece of knitting. The basic method is most commonly used, but other methods are suitable for certain projects.

Basic Method

1. Knit two stitches, pass the first stitch over the one closest to the tip of the needle.

2. Knit the next stitch on the left-hand needle, pass the first stitch on the right-hand needle over the stitch just knitted.

3. Continue to the end of the row until you have one stitch remaining, cut the yarn, pass the yarn end through the remaining stitch, and draw tight.

Decrease Bind-Off

1. Knit two stitches together, place the stitch on the right-hand needle back on the left-hand needle.

2. Repeat as above to the end of the row. Cut the yarn, pass the yarn end through the remaining stitch, and draw tight.

Three-Needle Bind-Off

This is used for joining two pieces of knitting, usually at a shoulder seam, and involves three knitting needles.

1. Place the two pieces of knitting together, with the wrong sides facing, holding the two knitting needles in the left hand with the points facing the same way. Insert the tip of the right-hand needle (the third needle) into the first stitch on each of the left-hand needles. Knit these two stitches together and place the new stitch on the right-hand needle.

2. Insert the tip of the right-hand needle into the first stitch on each of the left-hand needles. Knit these two stitches together and place the new stitch on the right-hand needle.

3. Pass the first stitch on the right-hand needle over the stitch just knitted.

4. Continue to the end of the row until you have a neat ridge of bound-off stitches and one stitch remaining. Cut the yarn, pass the end through the remaining stitch, and draw tight.

Basic Stitches

Knit Stitch

This is the most basic of stitches. After casting on, proceed as follows:

1. Place the tip of the right-hand needle in the first stitch on the left-hand needle, going through from left to right.

2. Taking the yarn behind the right-hand needle, bring it through between the two needle tips and pull the loop through with the right-hand needle. This loop on the right-hand needle is the new stitch.

3. Drop the original loop from the left-hand needle.

4. Continue working in this way to the end of the row until all the stitches are on the right-hand needle.

Purl Stitch

1. Bring the yarn to the front of the work. Insert the right-hand needle tip in the first stitch on the left-hand needle from right to left.

2. Wrap the yarn between the two needle tips and around to the front of the right-hand needle.

3. Pull the loop through onto the right-hand needle to make a stitch and let the loop drop from the left-hand needle.

4. Continue working in this way to the end of the row until all the stitches are on the right-hand needle.

Stockinette Stitch

This is a smooth stitch with a right side and a wrong side. It is formed by working one row in knit and one row in purl. The knit side is the right side of work.

Reversed Stockinette Stitch

This is exactly the same as stockinette stitch, but the purl side is the right side of the work.

Garter Stitch

This is a ridged stitch that will not curl at the edges and is suitable for borders and scarves. It is formed by working every row in knit.

Seed Stitch

This forms a textured stitch that will not curl.

Row 1: Work as a 1x1 rib to the end of row.

Row 2: If you ended the previous row with K1, begin this row with K1. If you ended the previous row with P1, begin this row with P1.

Rib

This is an elastic border that is commonly used for welts and cuffs on garments.

1x1 Rib: With the yarn at the back of the work, knit one stitch, bring the yarn to the front of work and purl one stitch. These two stitches are repeated to the end of the row.

2x2 Rib: With the yarn at the back of work, knit two stitches, bring the yarn to the front of the work and purl two stitches. Repeat to the end of the row.

Cable

Cabling is a method of crossing the stitches to form a textured design. There are various methods, and special abbreviations will be given in individual patterns. A number of stitches are placed on a cable needle and held at the back or front of the work. A similar number of stitches are knitted from the left-hand needle, and then the stitches from the cable needle are knitted.

Beading

Thread the beads onto the yarn before casting on. Thread a fine sewing or beading needle with sewing thread, and tie the ends of the thread to form a loop. Place the end of the knitting yarn through this loop, thread the beads onto the needle, and push down on to the knitting yarn. Continue until enough beads have been threaded to complete the design.

When a pattern indicates to place a bead on the knitting, bring the yarn with a bead to the front of the work, push the bead so that it is tight against the needle, slip the next stitch, take the yarn to the back of the work, and knit the next stitch.

Fair isle

Fair isle is a method of working in color by weaving the yarn not in use at the back of the work. The colors are changed every few stitches, but there are usually no more than two or three different colors to a row.

Intarsia

Intarsia is a method of working large blocks of color. To stop tangles forming, small lengths of yarn are wound onto bobbins. When a color is changed, the yarns are crossed at the back of the work to prevent a hole forming.

I-Cord

An i-cord is worked on two double-pointed needles in knit stitch over a small number of stitches. When the end of the row is reached, and without turning the needle, push the stitches to the other end of the needle and, keeping the yarn at the back of the work, knit another row. Continue without turning the needle until the cord is the required length. Stretch slightly to close up the gap.

Joining Pieces

Grafting

This forms an invisible seam between two pieces of knitting along an edge that would have been bound off.

Lay the two pieces of knitting with the edges to be grafted meeting and the right side facing up. Thread a needle with the knitting yarn, slip a few stitches at a time off the knitting needle, and pass the sewing needle through the stitches from each piece as shown in Fig 1 to form a row of stitches.

Fig 1. Grafting

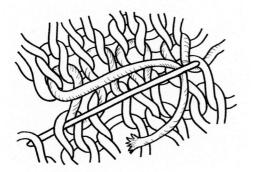

Mattress Stitch

This forms an invisible seam up the side edge of two pieces of knitting.

Lay the two pieces of knitting with the edges to be sewn meeting and right side facing up. Thread a needle with the knitting yarn and attach; place the needle under the bar of the first stitch on the right-hand piece of knitting, then under the bar of the first stitch on the left-hand piece of knitting. Continue up the seam, weaving in and out of the stitches as shown in Fig 2, and then pull the thread tight.

Fig 2. Mattress stitch

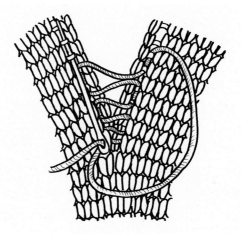

2

The Projects

Transform your home with this collection of stylish knits inspired by vintage patterns. These unique designs have been given a vintage look using period shades, natural fibers, and decorative touches such as glass beads and antique buttons. Rather than focusing on one particular era, these are timeless pieces that can be enjoyed by knitters of all ages and abilities, and they can all be customized to suit your style.

NECKLACE

THE INSPIRATION FOR THIS SOPHISTICATED NECKLACE came from a piece of anchor braid rope; the subtle twisting of the strands forms a soft, tactile chain. Knitting an i-cord is one of the easiest things to do. This simple tube can be achieved by novice knitters and is useful in many designs.

To completely transform the look of the necklace, try knitting each strand in a different shade. Use soft neutral colors for winter wear, or bright turquoise, green, and coral to complement a summer outfit. Using a thicker yarn will create a chunkier look. You could make the necklace long enough to slip over your head, joining the ends instead of using a bead fastening.

MATERIALS:

- Rowan Cotton Glace 100% mercerized cotton (125 yd/ 115 m per 50-g ball): 1 x 50-g ball pale gray
- Pair of 3.25-mm (US 3, UK 10) double-pointed needles
- 3.25-mm (D3) crochet hook
- Round bead (circumference approx. 2.5 in [5 cm])

GAUGE:

23 sts and 32 rows to 4 in (10 cm) over st st using 3.25-mm needles

FINISHED MEASUREMENTS:

After braiding, the necklace will measure approx. 19 in (48 cm) in length, not including bead or loop.

Using an old wooden bead for the fastener complements the colors and enhances the vintage look, but you can use whatever you like.

SMALL I-CORD (MAKE 4)

Using 3.25-mm double-pointed needles, cast on 4 sts.

*Knit one row. Without turning the needle, slide the sts to the other end of the needle, bring the yarn around the back of the sts, and k the next row.

Cont from * until work measures 24 in (61 cm)**.

Next row: Sl 1, k3tog, psso. Fasten off.

LARGE I-CORD (MAKE 1)

Leaving a tail of approximately 20 in (51 cm) and using 3.25-mm double-pointed needles, cast on 5 sts.

Work as for small i-cord from * to **.

Next row: Sl 1, k4tog, psso. Fasten off.

RIBBON FASTENING

Instead of using a bead to fasten the necklace, sew all the ends into each i-cord, cut a piece of ribbon into two lengths of approximately 12 in (31 cm), and attach the ribbons to each end of the necklace using a fine needle and sewing thread. Fasten in a bow.

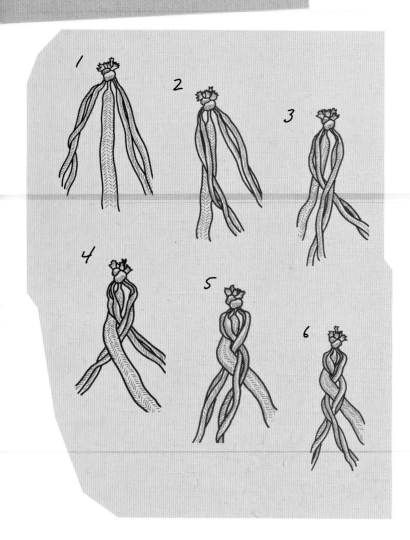

FINISHING UP

Place all the cast-on ends of the five cords together and tie a loose knot to keep them in place. Fasten this end to the back of a chair or get someone to hold it. Make a three-strand braid using two lots of the 2 small i-cords and the one large i-cord (see illustration).

When the braid is completed, hold the bound-off ends together tightly and join them neatly by overstitching each cord to the next one. Thread as many of the ends as possible through the hole in the bead (or other fastener) and knot tightly. Oversew the ends a few times into the knot to secure the fastener firmly, and cut off any remaining loose ends.

Undo the knot at the cast-on ends and oversew each cord to the next one as before. Pass 4 of the loose ends down through the center of the cords and cut, leaving the longest tail end. With the crochet hook, make a chain of 20 sts. Fold this over to make a loop and fasten off the end securely.

BATH MAT

THIS COOL CHUNKY BATH MAT IS KNITTED from a mixture of knitting yarn and recycled fabric. The knitting is enhanced by knotted strips of roughly torn fabric to give the mat a lovely organic texture. This is a fun project suitable for any level of experience and a very eco-friendly way to use up old clothing and towels.

For an extra-firm mat, back it with a piece of terry cloth fabric. This will absorb far more moisture and make it easier to wash and dry. Jazz it up with patterned fabric from old shirts, mixed with brightly colored knitting yarn—you can even use a few lengths of ribbon to incorporate yet another texture. If you prefer a smoother finish, push all the knots through to the back side of the mat when you have completed it.

MATERIALS:

- Debbie Bliss Cotton Double knitting 100% cotton (92 yd/84 m per 50-g ball): 3 x 50-g balls shade Stone (A)
- Approx. 500 g recycled fabric (B)
- Pair of 10-mm (US 14, UK 000) needles
- Pair of 12-mm (US 15, UK N/A) River John swing needles or a long circular needle

GAUGE:

6.5 sts and 9 rows to 4 in (10 cm) over g st using 12-mm needles

FINISHED MEASUREMENTS:

Approx. 17 x 27 in (43 x 68 cm)

Recycle things like T-shirts, cotton rags, calico, and towels for the fabric, and make the strips as long as possible.

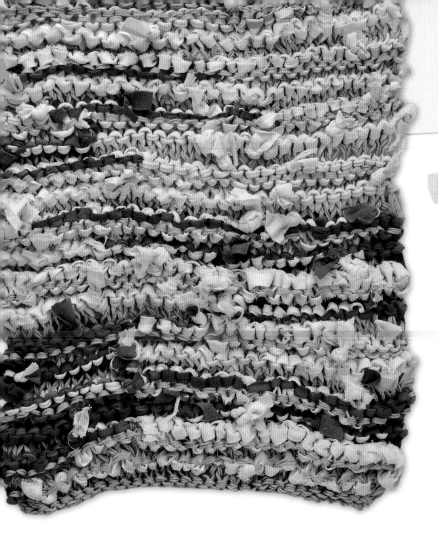

PREPARATION

Tear the fabric into long strips measuring approximately 1 in (2.5 cm) wide, and then knot them together to form a single length of "yarn." You can knot all of the fabric at once and wind it into a huge ball, or just do some initially and then add on more lengths as required as you go along.

MAT

Using 10-mm needles and 3 strands of yarn A, cast on 30 sts.

Rows 1–2: K.

Without breaking the yarn, change to the 12-mm swing needles and cont as follows:

Row 3: Using yarn B, k.

Row 4: Using yarn B, k.

Row 5: Using yarn A, k.

Remove the stopper from the end of the needle and place on opposite end without turning work.

Row 6: Using yarn B, k.

Row 7: Using yarn B, k.

Row 8: Using yarn A, k.

Cont to work 2 rows using yarn B and 1 row using yarn A without breaking the yarn. When the next shade to be used is at the opposite end of the row, remove the stopper from the swing needle, place on the opposite end, and cont working without turning the needle.

Cont until work measures 27 in (68 cm) ending with Row 4.

Change to 10-mm needles and work 2 rows in yarn A. Bind off.

FINISHING UP

Weave in any loose ends. Trim the knots and, if preferred, push through to the WS of mat.

Choose colors that coordinate with your home
furnishings. A vibrant red or pink with a black
silhouette would look equally effective.

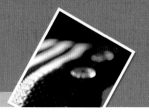

SILHOUETTE CUSHION

THIS STRIKING DESIGN IS CREATED from a simple stockinette-stitch cushion cover appliquéd with a silhouette cut out from a piece of felt. You can use the silhouette shown in the pattern, cut one out of a magazine, or make your own of someone you know—perhaps a family member or even a favorite pet. Classic silhouettes are black, but change the colors if preferred, or even stick to black but use colored thread in a satin stitch around the silhouette to coordinate with the color of the buttons.

There are various ways to make a silhouette. One of the easiest is to take an image with a digital camera. Place a bright light behind the subject and make them stand or sit sideways to the camera, so the profile is clear. Print the image and cut around the profile, then use this as a template for the fabric silhouette. Another method is to get your subject to sit perfectly still, place a light so that it casts a shadow on a wall, tape a piece of paper where the shadow falls, and carefully draw around the shadow.

MATERIALS:

- Rowan Handknit Cotton 100% cotton (93 yd/85 m per 50-g ball): 3 x 50-g balls Black (A); 3 x 50-g balls White (B)
- Pair of 4-mm (US 6, UK 8) needles
- 5 x buttons
- 16 x 16 in (40 x 40 cm) cushion pad
- Piece of black felt fabric measuring 12 x 12 in (30 cm x 30 cm)
- Black sewing thread (fine gauge suitable for use with a sewing machine)

GAUGE:

20 sts and 28 rows to 4 in (10 cm) over st st using 4-mm needles

FINISHED MEASUREMENTS:

16 x 16 in (40 x 40 cm)

TIP

There are various computer programs for creating silhouettes from digital images. The choice is yours!

CUSHION

Using shade A, cast on 80 sts.

Row 1: K1, p1 to end of row.

Row 2: P1, k1 to end of row.

Rows 3–6: Rep rows 1–2 (twice).

Row 7: (K1, p1) 3 times, *p2tog, yrn over twice, sl 1, p1, psso, (k1, p1) 6 times**, rep from * to ** 4 times, p2tog, yrn over twice, sl 1, p1, psso, k1, p1 to end of row.

Row 8: (P1, k1) 3 times, p1, *k into front of first yo, p into back of second yo, (k1, p1) 7 times**, rep from * to ** 4 times, k into front of first yo, p into back of second yo, k1, p1 to last st, k1.

Rows 9–12: Rep rows 1 and 2.

Next row (RS): Change to shade B and beg with a k row cont in st st for 4 rows.

Next row: Change to shade A and cont in st st, changing the color every 4 rows until work measures 16 in (40 cm) from cast-on edge, ending with the 4th row (WS) of a stripe.

Next row: Using shade A, k1, p1 to end of row.

Next row: P1, k1 to end of row.

Rep the last 2 rows (5 times).

Bind off.

SILHOUETTE

Enlarge or reduce your image to approximately
9 x 9 in (23 x 23 cm). Cut out a paper template
and pin this to the felt fabric. Carefully cut out
the silhouette from the felt. Center this on the
cushion front approximately 2 in (5 cm) above
the buttonhole band and tack in place. St all the
way around the silhouette in satin st. Fasten off
any loose ends.

FINISHING UP

Place the knitted cover WS facing down on a table
with the buttonhole band at the top. Fold the top
three-quarters of the cover down so that the RS
are together. Fold the bottom quarter up so that
the button band lays on top of the buttonhole
band. St both side seams, matching all the
stripes. Turn RS out and sew the buttons on the
button band to correspond with the holes.

KNITTING NEEDLE ROLL

THIS PRACTICAL YARN AND FABRIC ROLL will store up to ten pairs of knitting needles. The softly draping exterior is knitted in a stripe-and-eyelet design, then lined with coordinating fabric. The simple lining is machine stitched and then sewn in place by hand—a project that can be undertaken by novice knitters with little or no experience of sewing.

I have chosen a plain shade for the lining, but if you want to jazz it up, choose a patterned or striped fabric in complementary shades. If you are a confident seamstress, why not add another shorter row of pockets on top of the knitting needle pockets to store double-pointed needles?

MATERIALS:

- Rowan Lenpur Linen 75% VI Lenpur, 25% linen (125 yd/115 m per 50-g ball): 2 x 50-g balls Green (A); 1 x 50-g ball Purple (B); 1 x 50-g ball Lime (C)
- Pair of 4-mm (US 6, UK 8) needles
- 60 in (152 cm) of ½-inch (12-mm)-wide ribbon in a corresponding color
- 40 x 24 in (100 x 61 cm) piece of lining fabric
- Green sewing thread (fine guage suitable for use with a sewing machine)

GAUGE:

22 sts and 30 rows to 4 in (10 cm) over st st using 4-mm needles

FINISHED MEASUREMENTS:

Approx. 21 x 17 in (55 x 45 cm)

Add more color and texture by threading ribbon through the eyelet rows. Fasten at each end before sewing in the lining.

KNITTED EXTERIOR

Using shade A, cast on 89 sts.

1st row: K1, p1 to end of row.

Rep this row 3 more times.

Beg with a k row, cont in st st working stripe patt as follows:

Rows 1–16: A.

Row 17: B.

Row 18: Using B, k1, *yfwd, k2tog, k2; rep from * to end.

Rows 19–20: B.

Rows 21–26: A.

Rows 27–29: C.

Rows 30–31: B.

Row 32: Using B, k1, *yfwd, k2tog, k2; rep from * to end.

Row 33: B.

Rows 34–35: C.

Rows 36–39: A.

Rows 40–45: C.

Rows 46–62: A.

Row 63: B.

Row 64: Using B, k1, *yfwd, k2tog, k2; rep from * to end.

Rows 65–66: B.

Rows 67–72: C.

Rows 73–77: B.

Row 78: Using B, k1, *yfwd, k2tog, k2; rep from * to end.

Rows 79–83: B.

Rows 84–98: A.

Rows 99–103: C.

Row 104: B.

Row 105: Using B, k1, *yfwd, k2tog, k2; rep from * to end.

Rows 106–107: B.

Row 108: C.

Rows 109–110: A.

Rows 111–116: C.

Rows 117–150: A.

Row 151: Using A, k1, p1 to end of row.

Rep row 151 (3 more times).

Bind off.

FINISHING UP

With RS facing and using shade A, pick up and k 119 sts evenly along one long edge (to space the sts evenly *pick up and k one st on 3 consecutive rows, then skip one row, rep from * to end of row until you have 119 sts or a similar odd number of sts).

Next row: K1, p1 to end.

Rep last row (4 times) to form seed st edge.

Rep the previous steps on the other side edge.

Thread the ribbon through the center 4 eyelets of the eyelet row second from the top, and using a sewing thread lightly st in place.

Sew in any loose ends and pin and block into shape.

LINING

Using the knitted piece as a size guide, cut out one piece of fabric the same size and a smaller piece of fabric the same width along the base and top, but measuring only 13 in (33 cm) long.

Turn over a hem of ½ in (1.2 cm) along the top edge of each piece. Press and stitch them.

Place the 2 pieces of fabric RS together, with the base of each piece flush, leaving a ½ in (1.2 cm) seam allowance. Pin, and st down the 2 sides and across the base.

Fold the 2 raw edges of the larger piece of fabric into the WS of work so that they are in line with the seams you have created in step 2; press and seam.

Turn the fabric RS out. Using pins, mark a vertical line from the top to the base of the smaller piece of fabric to indicate 10 pockets for the knitting needles; these can all be the same size or you can increase them slightly for larger needles. I have made 6 x 1½ in (15 x 4 cm) and 4 x 2 in (10 x 5 cm) pockets.

St a vertical line indicated by each line of marker pins to make the pockets.

FINISHING UP

Place the knitted piece and the lining fabric WS together and, with a fine sewing thread, neatly slip st the lining fabric in place along the ridge between the st st and seed st border.

Your project is now ready to fill with knitting needles. The top flap folds over to stop them falling out; roll up the bundle and fasten with a bow.

Stages 1 & 2

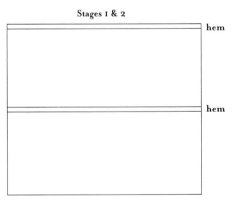

hem

hem

Stage 3

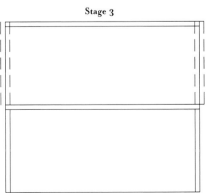

PROJECT 5

HEADBAND

THIS RETRO HEADBAND HAS A 1930S APPEAL; the warm band fits snugly over the ears and is decorated with a large knitted flower. This easy project can be completed by most skill levels and makes a lovely gift.

Experiment by working the flower in brighter multicolored shades or use up yarn oddments to stripe the petals. For a bolder look, make two or three flowers in different sizes and group them together so that they overlap. Make the headband sparkle by adding beads or sequins to the knitted flowers and use a silk yarn in black or pewter for sophisticated party wear.

MATERIALS:

- Debbie Bliss Rialto Aran 100% merino wool (87 yd/ 80 m per 50-g ball): 1 x 50-g ball Paprika (A)
- Fleece Artist Woolie Silk 3-ply 65% wool, 35% silk (252 yd/230 m per 100-g skein): 1 x 100-g skein Madder (B)
- Pair each of 4-mm (US 6, UK 8) and 5-mm (US 8, UK 6) needles
- 1 x button

GAUGE:

Rialto Aran: 22 sts and 18 rows to 4 in (10 cm) over rib pattern using 5-mm needles. Woolie Silk 3-ply: 20 sts and 32 rows to 4 in (10 cm) over st st using 4-mm needles

FINISHED MEASUREMENTS:

Headband approx. 20 in (51 cm) circumference without stretching

You could replace the
button in the middle of
the flower with a cluster
of embroidered French
knots in a silk thread.

ABBREVIATIONS

K1b—k 1 st from the row below.

HEADBAND

Cast on 21 sts using shade A and 5-mm needles.

Row 1: P.

Row 2: P1, *p1, k1b, rep from * to last 2 sts, p2.

Rep last 2 rows until work measures 20 in (51 cm) ending with a P row.

Bind off.

FLOWER

Small circle:

Using shade B and 4-mm needles, cast on 60 sts.

Row 1 (RS): K.

Row 2 and every alt row: P.

Row 3: *K3, k2tog; rep from * to end (48 sts).

Row 5: *K2, k2tog; rep from * to end (36 sts).

Row 7: *K1, k2tog; rep from * to end (24 sts).

Row 9: K2tog to end (12 sts).

Row 10: P.

Thread yarn through rem sts and pull tight. Sew up seam.

Large circle:

Using shade B and 4-mm needles, cast on 60 sts.

Row 1: K.

Row 2: P.

Rows 3–4: Rep rows 1–2.

Row 5: *K3, k2tog; rep from * to end (48 sts).

Row 6: P.

Rows 7–8: Rep rows 1–2.

Row 9: *K2, k2tog; rep from * to end (36 sts).

Row 10: P.

Rows 11–12: Rep rows 1–2.

Row 13: *K1, k2tog; rep from * to end (24 sts).

Row 14: P.

Rows 15–16: Rep rows 1–2.

Row 17: K2tog to end (12 sts).

Row 18: P.

Thread yarn through rem sts and pull tight. Sew up seam.

FINISHING UP

Join the 2 ends of the headband. With the seam
centered at the back of the headband, fasten the
flower just off the center front by placing the
smaller circle on top of the larger one. Attach
to the headband with the button in the center.

For a sleeker version, increase the number of stitches and knit with a fine mercerized cotton yarn.

LAMPSHADE

THIS GORGEOUS CHUNKY LAMPSHADE COVER will transform a plain or faded shade. The cool creamy color allows the light to shine through, but experiment with darker shades for different lighting effects.

The cover is very quick to knit in superchunky wool using large knitting needles; the simple chevron design is easy to work. The large natural buttons give a vintage look to the lamp. For an alternative, use brightly patterned buttons or make each button a different color.

MATERIALS:

- Rowan Big Wool 100% merino wool (87 yd/80 m per 100-g ball): 1 x 100g White Hot
- Pair of both 10-mm (US 15, UK 000) and 12-mm (US 17, UK N/A) needles
- 3 x buttons

GAUGE:

10 sts and 12 rows to 4 in (10 cm) over pattern using 12-mm needles

FINISHED MEASUREMENTS:

20 x 7 in (51 x 18 cm)

SPECIAL ABBREVIATIONS:

BC (back cross)—sl 1 st on to cable needle at back of work, k1, p1 from cn.
FC—front cross, sl 1 st on to cable needle at front of work, p1, k1 from cn.

LAMPSHADE

Using 10-mm needles, cast on 50 sts. Knit 2 rows.

Change to 12-mm needles.

Row 1 (RS): Sl 1, k1, yfwd, k2tog, p to last 4 sts, k4.

Row 2: Sl 1, k to end.

Row 3: Sl 1, k3, p4, *BC, FC, p6**, rep from * to ** (3 more times ending last repeat with p4 instead of p6), k4.

Row 4: Sl 1, k7, *p1, k2, p1, k6**, rep from * to ** (3 more times), k2.

Row 5: Sl 1, k3, p3, *BC, p2, FC, p4**, rep from * to ** (3 more times ending last repeat with p3 instead of p4), k4.

Row 6: Sl 1, k6, *p1, k4, p1, k4**, rep from * to ** (3 more times), k3.

Row 7: Sl 1, k3, p2, *BC, p4, FC, p2**, rep from * to ** (3 more times), k4.

Row 8: Sl 1, k5, *p1, k6, p1, k2**, rep from * to ** (3 more times), k4.

Row 9 (RS): Sl 1, k1, yfwd, k2tog, p to last 4 sts, k4.

Row 10: Sl 1, k to end.

Rep rows 3–10 once more.

Change to 10-mm needles.

Knit 2 rows. Bind off.

FINISHING UP

Sew in ends, pin, and block. Attach the three buttons to correspond with the buttonholes on the opposite band.

NOTE

This cover is designed to fit a cylindrical lampshade measuring approximately 7 in tall and 18½ in circumference (18 and 47 cm). If you want to increase the width of the lampshade, adding 10 sts and working one extra patt rep will give you an extra 4 in (10 cm). You can increase the height of the lampshade by 3 in (8 cm) if you repeat rows 3–10 again. Each chevron is approximately 4 in wide and 3 in tall (10 x 8 cm).

TIP

If you want to cover a conical lampshade, with the same circumference at the bottom but a smaller opening at the top, simply omit the first two buttonholes so that there is just one fastening at the top. Wrap the cover around the lampshade, crossing the two top corners, and sew the button in place to correspond with the buttonhole.

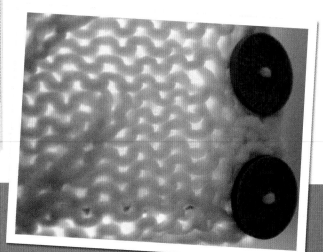

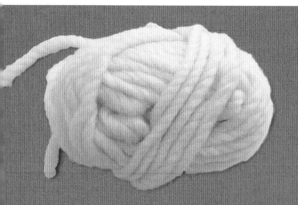

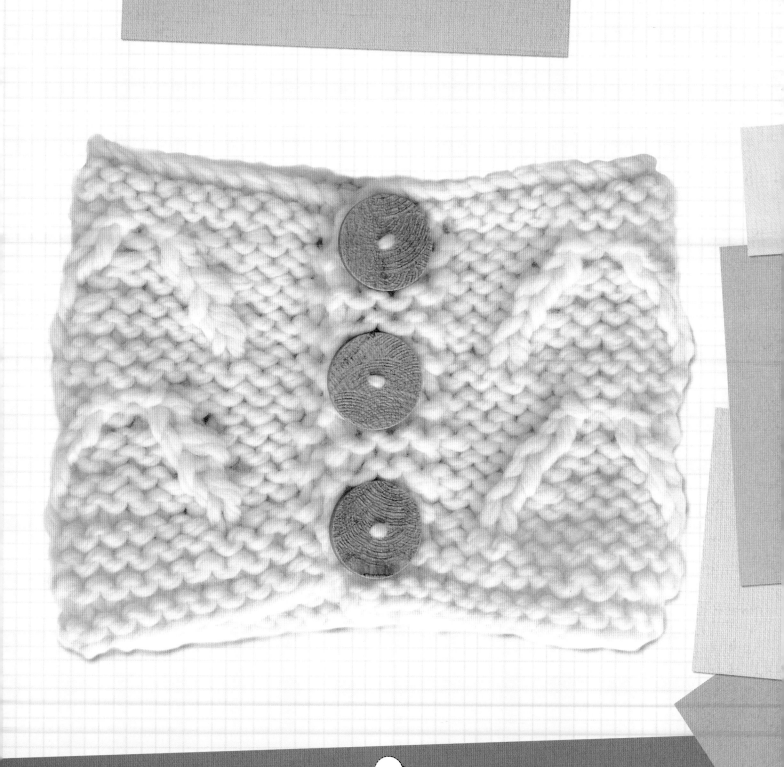

FAIR ISLE BAG

THIS HANDY LITTLE DRAWSTRING BAG was originally designed to carry a digital camera, but could be put to many uses. It is knitted in hard-wearing double-knit cotton using the fair isle method of weaving the yarn at the back of the work. A knitted i-cord keeps the bag firmly closed.

Fair isle knitting is a method of changing color every few stitches—full details of how to do this can be seen in the techniques section (see page 16). The look of a fair isle design can be changed dramatically by swapping the colors around; experiment with dark shades on a light background or bright, vivid shades on a dark background.

MATERIALS:

- Rowan Handknit Cotton 100% cotton (93 yd/85 m per 50-g ball): 2 x 50-g balls Blue (A); 1 x 50-g ball Pale Pink (B); 1 x 50-g ball (C) Stone; 1 x 50-g ball Pale Blue (D)
- 4-mm (US 6, UK 8) circular needle (short length)
- Set of 4-mm (US 6, UK 8) double-pointed needles

GAUGE:

22 sts and 25 rows to 4 in (10 cm) over fair isle pattern using 4-mm needles

FINISHED MEASUREMENTS:

Height from base 9 in (23 cm); circumference 14 in (36 cm)

If the main fair isle band is coming out tighter than the rest of the knitting, change to a 4.55-mm needle for rows 12 to 28 of the chart.

HOW TO MAKE AN I-CORD

Using a pair of double-pointed needles, cast on the required number of sts. *Knit one row, without turning the needle slide the stitches to the other end of the needle, bring the yarn around the back of the stitches and knit the next row.

Cont from * until the cord is the required length.

BAG

Using shade A and the circular needle, cast on 70 sts. Use a st marker to indicate the end of each round.

Round 1: K.

Round 2: *K1, yfwd, k3, sl 1, k2tog, psso, k3, yfwd, rep from * to end of round.

Round 3: K.

Round 4: *P1, k1, yfwd, k2, sl 1, k2tog, psso, k2, yfwd, k1, rep from * to end of round.

Round 5: *P1, k9, rep from * to end of round.

Round 6: *P1, k2, yfwd, k1, sl 1, k2tog, psso, k1, yfwd, k2, rep from * to end of round.

Round 7: *P1, k9, rep from * to end of round.

Round 8: *P1, k3, yfwd, sl 1, k2tog, psso, yfwd, k3, rep from * to end of round.

Round 9: *P1, k9, rep from * to end of round.

Next 2 rounds: K.

Next round: *K1, yfwd, k2tog, rep from * to last st, k1.

Next round: K.

Next round: *K11, m1; rep from * to last 4 sts, k4 (76 sts).

Next round: K.

Next round: Beg with row 1 of chart, cont in st st changing colors as shown on the chart and working 19 sts rep 4 times from right to left of chart on every row until all 39 rows have been completed.

Next 2 rounds: K using shade A.

Next round: P.

SHAPE BASE

Round 1: *K17, sl 1, k1, psso, rep from * to end of round (72sts).

Round 2: *K16, sl 1, k1, psso, rep from * to end of round (68 sts).

Round 3: *K15, sl 1, k1, psso, rep from * to end of round (64 sts).

Round 4: *K14, sl 1, k1, psso, rep from * to end of round (60 sts).

Round 5: *K13, sl 1, k1, psso, rep from * to end of round (56 sts).

Change to double-pointed needles and divide the sts evenly over 3 needles. Cont to dec 4 sts on every round, working one st less between each dec until there are 4 sts remaining. Thread yarn through these 4 sts and fasten off.

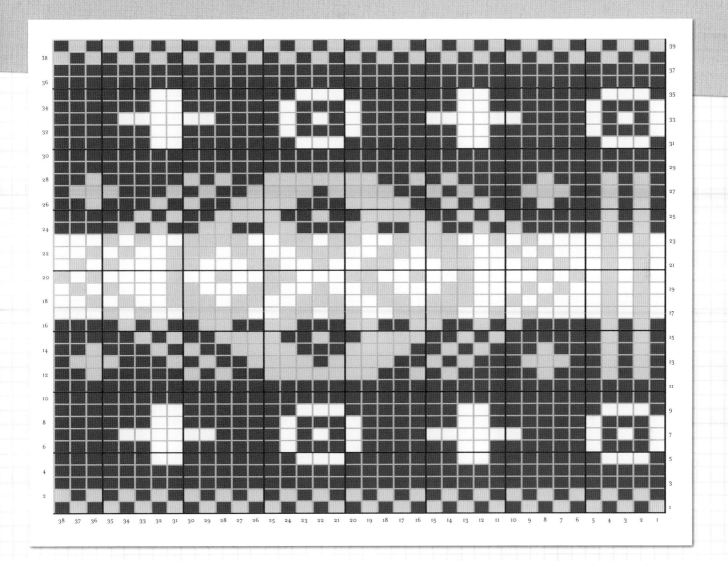

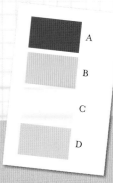

FINISHING UP

Sew in any loose ends and block.

I-CORD

Using 4-mm double-pointed needles and shade A, cast on 4 sts, make a cord measuring 28 in (71 cm), k2tog (twice), thread yarn through rem 2 sts, fasten off.

Thread cord through the eyelets and tie in a bow.

NOTE

To increase the strength of the bag, make a fabric lining for it; this could be in a pretty floral design or simple denim. Cut one piece of fabric to measure 15 x 8 in (38 x 20 cm) and a circular piece of fabric ½ in (13 mm) larger than the knitted base.

1. Fold the rectangular strip of fabric in half (RS together) and stitch the seam to form a tube. Press the seam flat.

2. Place the circular base at one end of the tube (RS facing into the tube) and pin in place. Snip small cuts all the way around the selvedge, from the edge to the pins, so that the base sits in the tube properly, then st in place.

3. Turn outward and st a small hem along the top edge of the tube; place inside the bag and slip st in place just underneath the eyelets.

CELL PHONE COVER

THIS CUTE LITTLE CASE FOR YOUR CELL PHONE will keep it safe from scratches and make it easy to find in your purse. The simple fair isle design is worked from a chart and knitted from side to side in stockinette stitch, with a garter stitch border.

The size of the design will fit most standard phones. To make it larger, either use a double-knit cotton and 4-mm (US 5, UK 8) knitting needles, or just add a couple of extra stitches at each end of the pattern row.

This is a quick project to knit, great for using up stash yarn, and makes a lovely gift.

MATERIALS:

- Rowan Cotton Glace 100% mercarized cotton (126 yd/115 m per 50-g ball): 1 x 50-g ball Umber (A); 5½–6½ yd (5–6 m) of each of the following: Lime (B); Orange (C); Pale Blue (D)
- 1 x button
- Pair of 3.25-mm (US 3, UK 10) needles
- 3.5-mm (E4) crochet hook
- 1 x button

GAUGE:

26 sts and 34 rows to 4 in (10 cm) over pattern using 3.25-mm needles

FINISHED MEASUREMENTS:

4½ x 3 in (11.5 x 7.5 cm)

Remember to weave the yarns at the back of the work every 3 sts to prevent holes forming in the design.

CELL PHONE COVER

Using shade A, cast on 30 sts.

Row 1: Sl 1, k to end of row.

Row 2: P to last 4 sts, k4.

Rows 3–4: Rep rows 1 and 2.

Next row: Sl 1, k4, starting at row 1 work patt rep from chart to the end of row.

Cont working from chart, keeping the garter st edging correct at beg of every k row and the end of every p row until the chart has been completed twice (48 rows from start of patt).

Bind off.

FINISHING UP

Sew in any loose ends. Pin and block. Fold the cover in half with RS together and join the cast-on and bound-off edges. Adjust it so that the seam lies down the center of the back and sew the short edge along the bottom. Turn RS out.

With the crochet hook, make a chain of 16 sts. Fasten each end of this chain on the seam at the back just inside the garter st edge. Attach the button to the front of the cover to correspond with the loop.

When you are knitting an intarsia design, don't forget to cross the yarn at the back of the work when changing colors.

TOTE BAG

THIS STURDY BAG CAN BE USED FOR SHOPPING, as a knitting bag, or simply for storage. The knitted exterior has a bold intarsia design of a head of broccoli (or it could be a tree!) knitted in a hand-dyed yarn, with the florets knitted in seed stitch to emphasize the texture. The main part of the bag is knitted in cotton and has been given a fabric lining for extra strength.

The intarsia method is a way of working two or more blocks of color without tangles and without holes.

To complete the intarsia design in this project, you will need two balls of yarn in the main shade and one ball of yarn in the contrast shade. When you start the intarsia design, work with yarn A up to the first stitch of the motif, join in yarn B and, using this shade only, work the stitches of the motif. Then change to the second ball of yarn A. See further details for intarsia knitting on page 16.

MATERIALS:

- Rowan Handknit Cotton 100% cotton (96 yd/85 m per 50-g ball): 6 x 50-g balls Navy (A)
- Hand Maiden Casbah 81% merino, 9% cashmere, 10% nylon (355 yd/325 m per 115-g skein): 1 x 115-g skein Moss (use two strands together) (B)
- Pair of 3.75-mm (US 5, UK 9) needles
- Piece of lining fabric 40 x 20 in (100 x 50 cm)
- Sewing thread in matching shades

GAUGE:

19 sts and 29 rows to 4 in (10 cm) over st st using 3.75-mm needles

FINISHED MEASUREMENTS:

14 in tall, 15 in wide, and 4 in deep across bottom (35.5 x 38 x 10 cm)

BACK

Cast on 73 sts using shade A.

Starting with a k row, cont in st st for 16 rows, ending with a WS row.

Cast on 11 sts at the beg of next 2 rows (95 sts). Cont in st st until work measures 15 in (38 cm) from bottom edge ending with a WS row.

Next row: K1, p1 to last st, k1.

This forms the first seed st row, rep last row 7 times. Bind off in seed st.

FRONT

Work as back until piece measures 6 in (15 cm) from cast-on edge, ending with a WS row.

Next row: K23, beg at row 1 work 49 sts of chart (see page 69), k23; complete all 60 rows of chart, reading the chart from right to left on odd rows and from left to right on even rows.

When the chart has been completed, cont in shade A and st st until work measures the same as back to seed st edging, ending with a WS row.

Next row: K1, p1, to last st, k1.

This forms the first seed st row, rep last row 7 times. Bind off in seed st.

HANDLES (MAKE 2 ALIKE)

Using shade A, cast on 9 sts.

Row 1: K1, p1 to last st, k1.

Rep row 1 until work measures 13 in (33 cm).

Bind off in seed st.

FINISHING UP

Sew in any loose ends. Pin and block into shape.

Using either the front or the back as a template, cut out 2 pieces of lining fabric to the same shape, allowing an extra ¼ in (0.5 cm) all around on the fabric for the seam. Do the same with the handles.

Put the fabric aside.

Place the front and back knitted pieces RS together and sew along the base seam (cast-on edge).

Sew down the 2 long side seams.

Flatten out the base seam so that the side seams and base seam meet in the middle of the small opening. Sew across this opening; rep at the other corner.

Turn RS out.

LINING

Turn a 1 in (2.5 cm) hem over to the WS along the top of the front, press, and stitch in place. Rep with the back.

Place the 2 pieces of fabric RS together; stitch the base seam and the 2 side seams. Press the seams flat.

With the base seam flat, match it so that the side seams and base seam meet in the middle of the small opening; sew across this opening. Rep at the other corner.

Place the lining inside the knitted bag.

HANDLES

Turn the raw edges under on each piece of lining fabric for the handles; press and stitch.

Slip stitch the linings to the knitted handles down each long edge. The short edges can be left unstitched.

Sandwich each end of the handles (knitted side facing out) between the lining fabric and the knitted bag, placing each end of the handle 7 in (18 cm) in from the side seam of the bag. Pin in place. Neatly sew the handle ends to the lining fabric (work 2 or 3 rows of stitching to give extra strength).

Slip stitch the top edge of the lining to the seed stitch edging of the bag all the way round. Slip stitch the seed stitch edging of the bag to the outside of the handles.

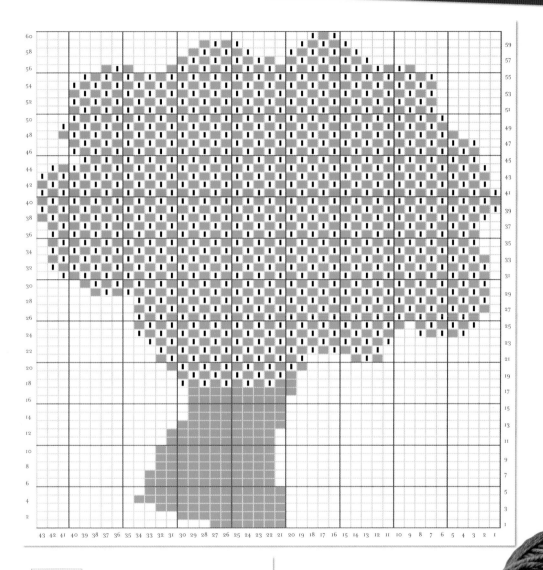

⬜	Shade A
🟦	Shade B K on RS, p on WS.
▐	Shade B P on RS, k on WS.

COFFEE PRESS WARMER

KEEP YOUR COFFEE WARM WITH THIS ELEGANT COVER. The soft fluffy yarn is knitted in a seed stitch and cable design, and is fastened with decorative buttons. This is a reasonably simple design to complete and would be a good introduction for knitters learning to cable. The yarn can be substituted with any standard double knit, but remember that wool, alpaca, and mohair will keep your coffee warmer for longer!

Change the color to suit your décor. If you want to use up oddments of yarn, make the button bands in a different color and use a mixture of odd buttons in various complementary shades.

MATERIALS:

- Rowan Baby Alpaca DK 100% baby alpaca (109 yd/100 m per 50-g ball): 2 x 50-g balls Taupe
- 6 x buttons
- Pair of 3.75-mm (US 5, UK 9) needles
- Cable needle

GAUGE:

26 sts and 28 rows to 4 in (10 cm) over cable pattern using 3.75-mm needles

FINISHED MEASUREMENTS:

To fit a coffee press with a jug that measures approx 7 in tall and 12 in circumference (18 x 31 cm). For a taller model, cont until work measures required length. For a larger circumference, increase the number of seed stitches worked at each end of the row in multiples of 2.

The buttons are an important feature of this design, so take care to choose something a little special.

SPECIAL ABBREVIATIONS:

C6F—place the next 3 sts on a cable needle at the front of work. K3, k3 from cable needle.

MAIN PART

Cast on 78 sts.

Row 1 (RS): K1, p1 (6 times), *k6, k1, p1, k1, p1, k1, p1, rep from * until 12 sts remaining, k1, p1 to end.

Row 2: P1, k1 (6 times), *p6, p1, k1, p1, k1, p1, k1, rep from * until 12 sts remaining, p1, k1 to end.

Row 3: K1, p1 (6 times), *C6F, k1, p1, k1, p1, k1, p1, rep from * until 12 sts remaining, k1, p1 to end.

Row 4: As row 2.

Row 5: As row 1.

Row 6: As row 2.

These 6 rows form the patt. Cont until work measures 6⅓ in (16 cm), finishing on either row 6 or row 2 of the patt. Bind off, keeping patt correct.

BUTTON BANDS (MAKE 3 ALIKE)

Cast on 5 sts.

Row 1: K1, p1 (twice), k1.

Rep until work measures 2 in (5 cm).

Next row: K1, p1, yon, k2tog, K1.

Next and following 2 rows: Rep row 1.

Bind off in seed stitch.

FINISHING UP

Pin and block. Sew in any loose ends.

Place the work flat on a surface with RS down.
Fold the right-hand edge toward the middle
and rep with the left-hand edge, leaving a gap of
approximately 1 in (2.5 cm) down the middle.

Space the 3 button bands evenly across the gap,
with the buttonhole on the left-hand side.
Fasten each button band in place on the right-
hand side by sewing on a button through the
band and the main piece. Sew the rem 3 buttons
in place down the opposite edge of the main
piece to correspond with the buttonholes on the
button bands.

The cover is now ready to wrap around your
coffee press—put the kettle on and relax with
a steaming hot cup of coffee.

TABLE MAT AND NAPKIN RING

THIS LOVELY MATCHING SET will give the dinner table a sophisticated finish, with the beaded knitting sparkling romantically in candlelight. The geometric design is created by knitting with small glass beads pre-threaded onto the cotton yarn. Beading is a simple and effective way of producing a truly special piece of knitting, changing the color of the yarn and giving unique results.

This project is suitable for intermediate knitters and is a good introduction to beading. Both pieces are knitted in stockinette stitch, with garter stitch edgings and picot hems at each end of the table mat.

TIP

Read the chart from right to left on the RS of work and from left to right on the WS of work.

MATERIALS:

Sufficient to make one table mat and one napkin ring:
- Rowan Cotton Glace 100% mercerized cotton (126 yd/ 115 m per 50-g ball): 2 x 50-g balls Blood Orange
- Pack of 500 Debbie Abrahams glass beads shade 39 Shell, size 6/0 (approximately 3 mm)
- Pair of 3.25-mm (US 3, UK 10) needles
- Beading needle and thread

GAUGE:

23 sts and 32 rows to 4 in (10 cm) over st st using 3.25-mm needles

FINISHED MEASUREMENTS:

Table Mat
9½ x 13 in (24 x 33 cm)

Napkin Ring
4¼ x 7½ in (11 x 19 cm)

You can change the table mat to a table runner by repeating the bead pattern until it is the required length.

SPECIAL ABBREVIATION

PB—place bead.

SPECIAL TECHNIQUES

To place a bead on the knitting, bring the yarn with a bead forward, slip the next st, place the bead in front of the slipped st, pushing it firmly in place, take the yarn to the back of work, and knit the next st.

PREPARATION

Before starting, thread the yarn with approximately 300 beads for one table mat (the table mat takes just over one ball of yarn, so it is advisable to thread all 300 on to one ball) and 60 beads for one napkin ring. See the techniques section (page 16) for details on how to thread the beads.

TABLE MAT

Cast on 59 sts.

Next row (RS): Sl 1, k to end of row.

Next row: Sl 1, p to end of row.

Rep these 2 rows once more.

Next row: *K2, yfwd, k2tog, rep from * to the last 3 sts, k3.

Next row: P.

Next 6 rows: K.

Next row (RS): Sl 1, k to end.

Next row: Sl 1, k4, p to last 5 sts, k5.

Next row: Starting with row 1 of 49-st chart and keeping the garter st edging correct, work rows 1–31 of the chart placing beads as shown.

After completing row 31 of the chart, cont to slip the first st of every row and, keeping the garter st edging correct, cont in st st commencing with a p row until work measures 4½ in (11 cm) from the last row of beading.

Next row: Starting with row 1 of 49-st chart and keeping the garter st edging correct, work rows 1–31 of the chart placing beads as shown.

Next row: Sl 1, p to last 5 sts, k5.

Next row: Sl 1, k to end.

Rep last row 5 times.

Next row: Picot row, *k2, yfwd, k2tog, rep from * to the last 3 sts, k3.

Next row: P.

Starting with a k row, work 4 rows in st st.

Bind off.

FINISHING UP

Sew in any loose ends. Turn each end under, making a fold line at the picot row, and slip st into place. Pin and block.

NAPKIN RING

Cast on 27 sts.

Row 1: Sl 1, k to end.

Row 2: Sl 1, k4, p to last 5 sts, k5.

Rep last 2 rows until work measures 1½ in (4 cm).

Working sts 1–17 only from the chart, cont as follows:

Next row: Sl 1, k4, beg at row 1, work st 1–17 of chart k5. Work rows 1–31 of chart keeping the garter st edging correct at each end of the row and slipping the first st on every row.

Next row: Sl 1, k4, p to last 5 sts, k5.

Next row: Sl 1, k to end.

Rep last 2 rows until work measures 1½ in (4 cm) from the end of beading, finishing with a WS row. Bind off.

FINISHING UP

Sew in any loose ends. Pin and block. Join the cast-on and bound-off edges.

NOTE

For extra protection, back the table mat with a piece of fabric. Simply cut a piece of fabric to measure ½ in (1.5 cm) more than the finished table mat, stitch a ½ in (1.5 cm) hem all the way around the piece of fabric, and slip stitch it into place on the back of the mat.

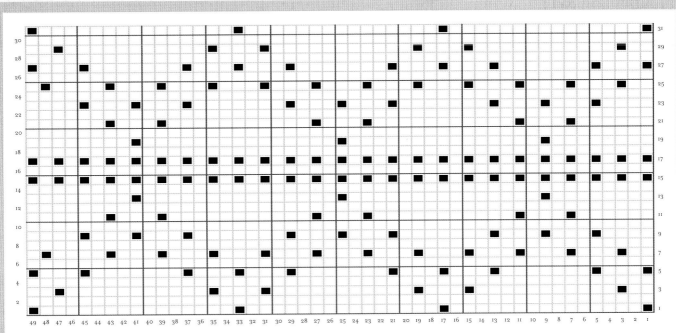

	Knit on RS, Purl on WS
■	PB

LACE CURTAIN

A SILKY LACE CURTAIN will dress up a window that is overlooked or has a view that you would prefer not to see. This delicate design is knitted in a beautiful hand-dyed silk blend. The decorative glass beading gives the curtain enough weight to help it hang straight and sparkles gently in the sunshine.

The curtain can be totally flexible in size; with a few easy adjustments to the pattern, it will fit any window. Choose between a café curtain that is fitted halfway up the window or create a long matching pair.

The width can be increased in blocks of 2 in (5 cm), by casting on multiples of 10 sts for every extra 2 in (5 cm) required. To increase the drop of the curtain, simply continue working the lace pattern until it is the required length.

MATERIALS:

Sufficient to knit the size shown in the pattern:
- Hand Maiden Sea Silk 70% silk, 30% sea cell (437 yd/400 m per 100-g skein): 1 x 100-g skein Ivory
- Pair of 4-mm (US 6, UK 8) needles
- Approx. 250 3-mm glass beads
- 9 x buttons

GAUGE:

20 sts and 30 rows to 4 in (10 cm) over lace pattern after blocking using 4-mm needles

FINISHED MEASUREMENTS:

15 in (38 cm) long, not including tabs x 17 in (43 cm) wide, after blocking

The beads will catch the light beautifully; just remember to thread enough beads onto the yarn before starting to knit!

SPECIAL ABBREVIATION

PB—place bead.

CURTAIN

Cast on 85 sts.

Rows I and 3 (WS): Sl I, p to end of row.

Row 2: Sl I, k4, *yfwd, kI, sl I, k2tog, psso, kI, yfwd, k5**, rep from * to ** to end of row.

Row 4: Sl I, kI, pb, k2, *yfwd, kI, sl I, k2tog, psso, kI, yfwd, k2, pb, k2**, rep from * to ** to end of row.

Rep rows I–4 until work measures I5 in (38 cm) or required length, ending on row 3 of patt. Leave the sts on the needle and cont as follows:

TABS

*Next row: Sl I, k4, turn.

Working on these 5 sts, rep previous row (3I times).

Next row: Sl I, kI, yfwd, k2tog, kI.

Next row: Sl I, k4.

Rep last row (4 more times). Bind off**.

Return to sts on LH needle, rejoin yarn and bind off 5 sts.

Counting the st remaining on RH needle as sl I on the first row, work from * to **.

Cont knitting the tabs and binding off between each tab until 9 tabs have been worked and you have reached the end of the row.

FINISHING UP

Gently stretch into shape so that the lace patt opens out to the given gauge; pin and block. Sew in all loose ends.

Attach a button to the base of each tab on the RS of work.

Your curtain is now ready for hanging. Wrap the tabs around the pole and fasten the buttons at the front.

NOTE

Experiment with different weights of yarn. Knit small gauge squares using larger needles and a thicker silk or cotton yarn. To create extra sparkle, place a bead on every alternate row instead of every fourth row. Alternatively, to block out more light, thread ribbon of a matching or contrasting shade down the lace eyelets.

Bobbles are easy to knit and create a lovely textured effect. Always make sure they are pushed through to the right side of the work and the gauge is kept firm and even.

WINE BOTTLE COVER

THIS SNUG-FITTING COVER WILL KEEP YOUR RED WINE WARM or, if you are giving a bottle as a gift, it makes the perfect wrap. The main part is decorated with a cable and bobble design that becomes a tight rib at the top to fit snugly over the neck of the bottle. It is designed to fit standard-sized 750-mL wine bottles.

The cozy wool and alpaca blend is ideal to keep red wine at the perfect temperature. If you want to make the cover to keep white or rosé wine cool, choose a light cotton yarn in pale or neutral shades. To complete a gift wrap, find a matching ribbon and tie it around the neck with a handwritten label.

MATERIALS:

- Rowan Felted Tweed Aran 50% merino wool, 25% alpaca, 25% viscose (95 yd/87 m per 50-g ball): 1 x 50-g ball Cassis
- Pair each of 4.50-mm (US 7, UK 7) and 5-mm (US 8, UK 6) needles
- Cable needle

GAUGE:

17 sts and 24 rows to 4 in (10 cm) over patt using 5-mm needles

FINISHED MEASUREMENTS:

12¾ in (32.5 cm) circumference x 11.5 in (29 cm) height

SPECIAL ABBREVIATIONS

MB—make bobble: K1, p1 (twice into next st), *turn, p4, turn, k4**, rep from * to **, turn, sl 1, p3tog, psso, turn, p1.

T3B—sl next st onto cn at back of work, k2, p1 from cn.

T3F—sl next 2 sts onto cn at front of work, p1, k2 from cn.

C5B—sl next 3 sts onto cn at back of work, k2, k3 from cn.

WINE BOTTLE COVER

Using 4.50-mm needles, cast on 48 sts.

Knit one row.

Next row: K12, m1, k1, m1, k22, m1, k1, m1, k12 (52 sts).

Change to 5-mm needles and work cable patt as follows:

Row 1 (RS): P10, *T3B, p1, T3F**, p18, rep from * to **, p10.

Row 2: K10, *p2, k3, p2**, k18, rep from * to **, k10.

Row 3: P9, *T3B, p1, MB, p1, T3F**, p16, rep from * to **, p9.

Row 4: K9, *p2, k5, p2**, k16, rep from * to **, k9.

Row 5: P8, *T3B, p5, T3F**, p14, rep from * to **, p8.

Row 6: K8, *p2, k7, p2**, k14, rep from * to **, k8.

Row 7: P7, *T3B, p7, T3F**, p12, rep from * to **, p7.

Row 8: K7, *p2, k9, p2**, k12, rep from * to **, k7.

Row 9: P6, *T3B, p1, MB, p5, MB, p1, T3F**, p10, rep from * to **, p6.

Row 10: K6, *p2, k11, p2**, k10, rep from * to **, k6.

Row 11: P6, *T3F, p9, T3B**, p10, rep from * to **, p6.

Row 12: K7, *p2, k9, p2**, k12, rep from * to **, k7.

Row 13: P7, *T3F, p7, T3B**, p12, rep from * to **, p7.

Row 14: K8, *p2, k7, p2**, k14, rep from * to **, k8.

Row 15: P8, *T3F, p2, MB, p2, T3B**, p14, rep from * to **, p8.

Row 16: K9, *p2, k5, p2**, k16, rep from * to **, k9.

Row 17: P9, *T3F, p3, T3B**, p16, rep from * to **, p9.

Row 18: K10, *p2, k3, p2**, k18, rep from * to **, k10.

Row 19: P10, *T3F, p1, T3B**, p18, rep from * to **, p10.

Row 20: K11, *p2, k1, p2**, k20, rep from * to **, k11.

Row 21: P11, C5B, p20, C5B, p11.

Row 22: K11, p5, k20, p5, k11.

Rows 23–24: Rep rows 21–22.

Rep rows 1–18.

Row 43: P4, p2tog, p4, *T3F, p1, T3B**, p3, p2tog, p8, p2tog, p3, rep from * to **, p4, p2tog, p4 (48 sts).

Row 44: K10, *p2, k1, p2**, k18, rep from * to **, k10.

Row 45: P4, p2tog, p4, C5B, p3, p2tog, p8, p2tog, p3, C5B, p4, p2tog, p4 (44 sts).

Row 46: K9, p5, k16, p5, k9.

Row 47: P4, p2tog, p3, C5B, p3, p2tog, p2, p2tog, p2, p2tog, p3, C5B, p3, p2tog, p4 (39 sts).

Row 48: K8, p5, k13, p5, k8.

Row 49: P4, p2tog, p2, k1, k3tog, k1, p3, p2tog, p3, p2tog, p3, k1, k3tog, k1, p2, p2tog, p4 (31 sts).

Row 50: K7, p3, k11, p3, k7.

Row 51: P2tog, p2, p2tog, p1, k3, p2, p2tog, p3, p2tog, p2, k3, p1, p2tog, p2, p2tog (25 sts).

Row 52: K5, p3, p9, p3, k5.

Row 53: P2tog, p1, p2tog, k3, p2tog, p1, p3tog, p1, p2tog, k3, p2tog, p1, p2tog (17 sts).

Row 54: K3, p3, k5, p3, k3.

Row 55: P3, k3, p1, p3tog, p1, k3, p3 (15 sts).

Row 56: K3, p3, k3, p3, k3.

Row 57: P3, k3, p3, k3, p3.

Rep last 2 rows (7 times).

Bind off loosely, keeping patt correct.

FINISHING UP

Pin and block. Sew up side seam and sew in any loose ends.

BOOKMARK CUFF

FOR SOMETHING DIFFERENT, try a cuff instead of the standard bookmark. This marks the page securely and also makes a pretty cover for the book. By increasing the length and adding more buttons to the design, your cuff will fit any size book.

I have chosen a 4-ply yarn for this project so that the cuff isn't too bulky and fits neatly between the pages. Mercerized cotton is the perfect fiber with a crisp finish and soft sheen.

The buttons are an integral part of the design. Place as many as you want in a straight line down each of the three seed-stitch bands and increase the length of the cuff. This will enable the cuff to fit a much wider range of book sizes.

MATERIALS:

- Rowan Siena 4-ply, 100% mercerized cotton (150 yd/ 140 m per 50-g ball): 1 x 50-g ball of pale green
- Pair of 2.75-mm (US 2, UK 12) needles
- Cable needle
- 6 x buttons

GAUGE:

44 sts and 42 rows to 4 in (10 cm) over cable and seed st patt using 2.75-mm needles

FINISHED MEASUREMENTS:

3.5 x 20 in (9 x 51 cm) (increase the length to fit any size book)

Small pearly buttons that are flat and smooth are ideal for the bookmark cuff; you need something thin to keep a low profile.

SPECIAL ABBREVIATIONS

C6F—place the next 3 sts on a cable needle at the front of work. K3, k3 from cable needle.

C6B—place the next 3 sts on a cable needle at the back of work. K3, k3 from the cable needle.

BOOKMARK CUFF

Cast on 33 sts.

1st row: K1, p1 to last st, k1.

Rep this row 4 more times.

Next row: K1, p1 (5 times), m1, (k1, p1) 7 times, k1, m1, *p1, k1, rep from * to end of row (35 sts).

Row 1 (RS): *K1, p1 (twice), k1, p2, k6, p2, rep from * (once), k1, p1 (twice), k1.

Row 2: *K1, p1 (twice), k3, p6, k2, rep from * (once), k1, p1 (twice), k1.

Row 3: K1, p1 (twice), k1, p2, C6F, p2, (k1, p1) twice, k1, p2, C6B, p2, (k1, p1) twice, k1.

Row 4: Rep row 2.

Row 5: Rep row 1.

Row 6: Rep row 2.

These 6 rows form the patt; cont until work measures 19½ in (50 cm), ending with a RS row.

Next row: Patt 9, p2tog, patt 13, p2tog, patt 9 (33 sts).

BUTTON BAND

Row 1 (RS): K1, p1 to last st, k1.

Row 2: K1, p1 to last st, k1.

Row 3: K1, p1, yrn, p2tog, k1, (p1, k1) 4 times, p1, k1, p1, yrn, p2tog, k1, (p1, k1) 4 times, p1, k1, p1, yrn, p2tog, k1.

Rows 4–6: K1, p1 to last st, k1.

Bind off in seed st.

FINISHING UP

Pin and block. Sew in any loose ends. Place buttons as shown in the image. If you have made the cuff longer, space the extra buttons at regular intervals down each seed st panel.

FLOWERPOT CUFF

BRIGHTEN UP YOUR SCRUFFY OLD FLOWERPOTS with this gorgeous cover. The textured leaf design trails around the top of the cuff and is enhanced with matching ceramic buttons. Cover a series of pots in the same colored cuff or, for a real splash of color, give each one an individual shade.

The design can be adjusted to fit pots of different sizes. To increase the circumference of the pot by 3¼ in (8 cm), add one extra leaf pattern repeat; for a smaller pot, taking out one leaf pattern repeat will decrease the circumference by 3¼ in (8 cm).

MATERIALS:

- Rowan Handknit Cotton 100% cotton (93 yd/ 85 m per 50-g ball): 1 x 50-g ball Gooseberry
- 3 x buttons
- Pair of 4-mm (US 6, UK 8) needles

GAUGE:

20 sts and 28 rows to 4 in (10 cm) over st st using 4-mm needles

FINISHED MEASUREMENTS:

6 x 17 in (15 x 43 cm) around base and 20½ in (52 cm) around top. It will fit a flowerpot 8–10 in (20–25 cm) tall, with a circumference of 20 in (51 cm) at the top.

Don't forget that if you are increasing the size of the cover to fit a larger pot, you will need more yarn!

FLOWERPOT CUFF

Cast on 30 sts.

Work garter st button band as follows:

Slipping the first st on every row, work 3 rows in knit.

Next row: Sl 1, k2, bind off next 2 sts, *k until 9 sts on RH needle, bind off next 2 sts**, rep from * to **, k3.

Next row: Sl 1, k2, *cast on 2 sts, k9**, rep from * to ** (twice), cast on 2 sts, k3.

Slipping the first st on every row, work 3 more rows in knit.

LEAF PATTERN

Row 1 (RS): Sl 1, k2, p3, (k1, yfwd) twice, k1, p3, k to end (32 sts).

Row 2: Sl 1, k2, p15, k3, p5, k6.

Row 3: Sl 1, k2, p3, k2, yfwd, k1, yfwd, k2, p3, k to end (34 sts).

Row 4: Sl 1, k2, p15, k3, p7, k6.

Row 5: Sl 1, k2, p3, k3, yfwd, k1, yfwd, k3, p3, k12, turn, wrap 1.

Row 6: P12, k3, p9, k6.

Row 7: Sl 1, k2, p3, k4, yfwd, k1, yfwd, k4, k3, k6, turn, wrap 1.

Row 8: P6, k3, p11, k6.

Row 9: Sl 1, k2, p3, k5, yfwd, k1, yfwd, k5, p3, k1, turn, wrap 1.

Row 10: P1, k3, p13, k6.

Row 11: Sl 1, k2, p3, k13, p3, k to end (40 sts).

Row 12: Sl 1, k2, p15, k3, p13, k6.

Row 13: Sl 1, k2, p3, k1, skpo, k7, k2tog, k1, p3, k to end (38 sts).

Row 14: Sl 1, k2, p15, k3, p11, k6.

Row 15: Sl 1, k2, p3, k1, skpo, k5, k2tog, k1, p3, k to end (36 sts).

Row 16: Sl 1, k2, p15, k3, p9, k6.

Row 17: Sl 1, k2, p3, k1, skpo, k3, k2tog, k1, p3, k to end (34 sts).

Row 18: Sl 1, k2, p15, k3, p7, k6.

Row 19: Sl 1, k2, p3, k1, skpo, k1, k2tog, k1, p3, k to end.

Row 20: Sl 1, k2, p15, k3, p1, p3tog, p1, k6 (30 sts).

Rep last 20 rows 5 more times.

Next row: Sl 1, then k to end of row.

Rep last row 7 more times. Bind off.

FINISHING UP

Sew in any loose ends. Pin and block. Sew buttons onto button band to correspond with the buttonholes.

NOTE

These handmade ceramic leaf buttons are perfect for this design. If you can't find anything similar, choose buttons in a natural material like wood or coconut. Alternatively, to give your cover a truly personal touch, you could use plain buttons and then add a handpainted floral design in complementary colors.

For an even more luxurious effect, you could use a light organza ribbon for the ties at the top.

CHUNKY SOCKS

THESE REALLY COZY SOCKS ARE KNITTED IN A LUXURY FIBER and designed to be worn around the house. If you would prefer to wear them outdoors with boots or shoes, it would be a good idea to use a yarn with a small percentage of nylon to increase their durability. The size can easily be adjusted by increasing or decreasing the length of the foot between the heel and toe shaping.

Sock knitting is very addictive. Knitters with little experience are often put off by the thought of turning a heel, but it is actually very easy to achieve. Thick, chunky socks are a good starting point as they "grow" much quicker than traditional sock yarns and are lovely to wear.

MATERIALS:

- Debbie Bliss Fez 85% extra-fine merino, 15% camel (109 yd/100 m per 50-g ball): 4 x 50-g balls shade Cayenne
- 5-mm (US 8, UK 6) double-pointed needles or short circular needle
- 3 yd (2 m) of ribbon

GAUGE:

28 sts and 24 rows to 4 in (10 cm) over cable pattern using 5-mm needles

FINISHED MEASUREMENT:

Foot length from heel to toe: 8½ in (22 cm)

Leg length to base of heel: 15 in (38 cm)

C6F—place the next 3 sts on a cable needle at the front of work. K3, k3 from cable needle.

SOCK (MAKE 2)

Cast on 48 sts and divide over 3 double-pointed needles (16 sts on each needle).

1st round: *K2, p2, rep from * to end of round.

Rep 1st round 9 more times.

Next round: *K2, yrn, p2tog, rep from * to end of round; this forms the eyelets for the ribbon.

Next round: *K2, p2, rep from * to end of round.

Cont with cable patt as follows:

Round 1: *K6, p2, rep from * to end of round.

Rounds 2–3: As round 1.

Round 4: *C6F, p2, rep from * to end of round.

Rounds 5–9: As round 1.

Rep rounds 4–9 until work measures 14 in (36 cm), ending with round 6.

HEEL SHAPING

Sl the last st worked onto the next dpn.

1st row (RS): Sl 1, k16, k7 from the next dpn (24 sts on this dpn).

Split the remaining 24 sts so that there are 12 sts on each of the 2 remaining dpns.

Working backward and forward in rows on the dpn with 24 sts, cont as follows:

2nd row: Sl 1, p to end of row (24 sts).

Rep rows 1–2 (8 more times), then rep row 1, one more time.

Cont as follows:

Row 1 (WS): P14, p2tog, p1, turn.

Row 2: K6, sl 1, k1, psso, k1, turn.

Row 3: P7, p2tog, p1, turn.

Row 4: K8, sl 1, k1, psso, k1, turn.

Row 5: P9, p2tog, p1, turn.

Row 6: K10, sl 1, k1, psso, k1, turn.

Row 7: P11, p2tog, p1, turn.

Row 8: K12, sl 1, k1, psso, k1, turn.

Row 9: P13, p2tog, turn.

Row 10: K13, sl 1, k1, psso (14 sts).

With the spare needle, pick up and k 12 sts down the side of the heel, sl these 12 sts onto the needle with the heel shaping (26 sts on first dpn).

Continuing at round 7 of the cable pattern and keeping patt correct, work across the next 12 sts from each remaining dpns (24 sts on 2nd dpn).

Pick up and k 12 sts up the other side of the heel and k 7 from the first dpn (19 sts on 3rd and 1st dpns).

Cont as follows:

Round 1: K to last 3 sts on 1st dpn, k2tog, k1 (18 sts on 1st dpn).

Work round 8 of cable pattern across 24 sts on 2nd dpn.

K1, sl 1, k1, psso, k to end of row on 3rd dpn (18 sts on 3rd dpn).

Round 2: K18, keeping patt correct cable 24, k18.

Rep last 2 rounds until you have 11 sts on 1st dpn, 24 sts on 2nd dpn, and 11 sts on 3rd dpn.

Next round: K11, cable 24, k11.

Cont working this round until work measures 6½ in (17 cm) from heel (or to fit your foot, allowing a further 2 in [5 cm] for toe shaping), ending with row 8 of cable patt and leaving 2 in (5 cm) for toe shaping.

TOE

Round 1: K to last 3 sts on 1st dpn, k2tog, k1.

K1, sl 1, k1, psso, k to last 3 sts on 2nd dpn, k2tog, k1.

K1, sl 1, k1, psso, k to end of 3rd dpn.

Round 2: K.

Rep rounds 1 and 2 until 22 sts remain. Split the sts so that there are 11 on each of 2 needles and graft the sts together.

FINISHING UP

Sew in any loose ends. Cut the ribbon into 2 x 5-ft (1.5-m) lengths and thread through the eyelet row at the top of the sock. Tie in a bow either at the outside edge of each sock or at the front.

HOT WATER BOTTLE COVER

THIS FUNKY COVER FOR A HOT WATER BOTTLE has a retro snowflake design knitted using the fair isle method of changing colors. The inspiration for this design came from an old ski sweater; the snug polo neck allows for easy filling of the bottle, and the cover fastens at the back with a row of buttons.

For this piece, I have chosen a wool and cashmere blend, which is soft to cuddle and easy to care for. Other good fiber choices would include alpaca or mohair blends. This project is suitable for intermediate knitters, and is easier to knit than it looks!

MATERIALS:

- Debbie Bliss Cashmerino Aran 55% merino wool, 33% microfiber, 12% cashmere (98 yd/90 m per 50-g ball): 2 x 50-g balls Pale Blue (A); 1 x 50-g ball Ecru (B); 1 x 50-g ball Terracotta (C)
- Pair of 5-mm (US 8, UK 6) knitting needles
- Pair of 5.5-mm (US 9, UK 5) needles
- 5 x buttons

GAUGE:

20 sts and 23 rows to 4 in (10 cm) over fair isle pattern using 5-mm needles

FINISHED MEASUREMENTS:

To fit a standard size hot water bottle: 9 in (23 cm) wide x 12 in (30 cm) long, not including cuff at top

To ensure the snowflake design is the same gauge as the rest of the knitting, change up to a 5.5-mm needle for rows 1 to 19 of the chart.

FRONT

*Using 5-mm needles and yarn A, cast on 17 sts. Starting with a k row, work 2 rows in st st.

Next row (WS): Cast on 5 sts, k to end (22 sts).

Next row: Cast on 5 sts, p to end (27 sts).

Chart row 1: Cast on 5 sts, beg on row 1 of chart A repeat the small snowflake pattern to the end of the row (32 sts).

Keeping patt correct across all the increases, work as follows:

Chart row 2: Cast on 5 sts, keeping patt correct p to end of row. (37 sts)**.

Cont in st st working the patt from chart A, inc 1 st at each end of the next 3 alt rows (43 sts).

Cont working from Chart A until you have repeated rows 1–8 4 times, ending with a WS row.

Next row (RS): Change to 5.5-mm needles. Using yarn A k2, starting with row 1 and first st of chart B, work the 20-st patt rep (twice), k1, inc 1 in last st (44 sts).

Keeping patt correct, cont to work in st st from chart B working 2 sts at each end of the row in yarn A until the 21 rows of the chart are completed, finishing on a RS row and dec 1 st at the end of the last row (43 sts).

Change to 5-mm needles. Starting with a WS row and reading row 1 of chart A from left to right work rows 1–6 of chart A.

Next row: Cont working from Chart A, at the same time bind off 6 sts at the beg of next 2 rows and 5 sts at the beg of foll 2 rows, keeping patt correct.

Leave rem 21 sts on a stitch holder.

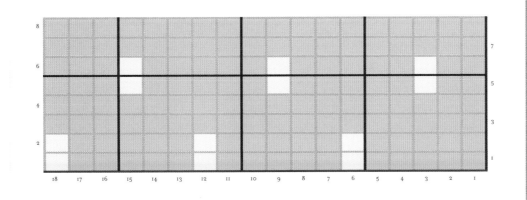

A

B

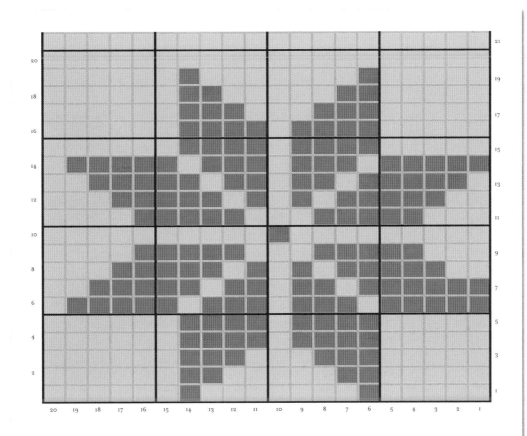

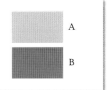

A

B

LOWER BACK

Work as front from * to **.

Cont in st st working the patt from Chart A until you have worked rows 1–8 3 times, at the same time inc 1 st at each end of next 3 alt rows (43 sts).

Work rows 1–2 from chart once more, inc 1 st at the end of last row (44 sts).

Using yarn A, work 4 x 4 rib as follows:

Next row (RS): K4, p4 to last 4 sts, k4.

Next row: P4, k4, to last 4 sts, p4.

Rep these 2 rows 2 more times. Bind off in rib.

UPPER BACK

Using 5-mm needles yarn A, cast on 44 sts.

Row 1 (RS): K4, p4 to last 4 sts, k4.

Row 2: P4, k4 to last 4 sts, p4.

Row 3: *K4, p1, bind off 2 sts, p1, rep from * to last 4 sts, k4.

Row 4: *P4, k1, cast on 2 sts, k1, rep from * to last 4 sts, p4.

Rep rows 1–2 once more.

Starting with a k row, work 2 rows in st st.

Change to 5.5-mm needles. Cont in st st working patt from Chart B for 21 rows. Dec 1 st at the end of final row of chart patt (43 sts).

Starting with a WS row and reading row 1 of chart A from left to right, work rows 1–6 of chart A.

Next row: Cont working from Chart A and, keeping patt correct, bind off 6 sts at the beg of next 2 rows and 5 sts at the beg of foll 2 rows.

Leave rem 21 sts on a spare needle.

NECK

Place the Front and Upper Back RS together and join one shoulder seam. Place the 42 sts back on a 5-mm needle and with the RS facing cont as follows:

Row 1: P2tog, p2, *k4, p4, rep from * to last 6 sts, k4, p2.

Row 2: K2, *p4, k4, rep from * to last 7 sts, p4, k3.

Rep rows 1–2 until rib measures 5 in (13 cm). Bind off in rib.

FINISHING UP

Pin and block. Sew in all the loose ends. With RS together sew the shoulder and side seams of the front and upper back. Place the lower back RS together with front so that it overlaps the button band of the upper back. Sew the side seams and base. With the hot water bottle cover inside out, join the neck rib seam with mattress stitch, turn the cover RS out and turn over the neck rib to form a cuff. Sew on buttons.

STAR COASTER

THESE FELTED COASTERS WILL PROTECT your tabletops from marking. The straightforward intarsia design is worked from a chart in stockinette stitch and then felted in the washing machine. Make a set of coasters all in the same color, or mix and match different shades.

For a simple, no-frills finish, work a row of single crochet around the edge of each coaster. If you want to make them stand out, edge with ribbon. To create Christmas coasters, knit them in seasonal shades and decorate with metallic ribbon.

MATERIALS:

- Debbie Bliss Andes 65% baby alpaca, 35% mulberry silk (109 yd/100 m to a 50-g skein): 1 x 50-g skein Purple (A); 1 x 50-g skein Gold (B)
- Pair of 4-mm (US 6, UK 8) needles
- 4-mm (G6) crochet hook
- 20 in (50 cm) ribbon per coaster (optional)

GAUGE:

22 sts and 30 rows to 4 in (10 cm) over st st before washing using 40-mm needles

FINISHED MEASUREMENTS:

5 x 5 in (13 x 13 cm) before washing at 122°F (50°C)

4 x 4 in (10 x 10 cm) after washing

When you wash the coaster, it's a good idea to pin it out on a piece of graph paper to ensure the sides stay exactly square.

Felting is an easy way of making a knitted piece feel firm. It will shrink and mat the fibers to give a solid fabric that doesn't stretch. When you are felting something in the washing machine, use a detergent and put something else in the wash that will cause a bit of friction—jeans or sneakers are both good to use. The degree of felting will vary with different washing machines, so it is always advisable to wash something on a lower temperature than suggested the first time as you can always wash it again if necessary.

COASTER

Using A, cast on 29 sts.

Commencing with a knit row and starting with row 1 of chart, cont in st st changing the colors as indicated until all 37 rows of the chart have been worked.

Bind off.

122

FINISHING UP

Sew in any loose ends. Machine wash at 122°F (50°C). Gently pull into a square shape, and pin out flat to dry.

CROCHET EDGING

Using the 4-mm crochet hook and shade A, work a border of single crochet around each edge, working 3 single crochet into each corner. Fasten off.

RIBBON EDGING

Cut the ribbon into 4 equal lengths, ½ in (12 mm) longer than each side of the square. Place the first piece of ribbon along one edge with the extra bit tucked under the coaster and, using a fine needle and thread, sew in place. Place the next piece of ribbon along so that it covers the raw end of the first piece, and then sew in place as before. Rep with the final 2 pieces of ribbon.

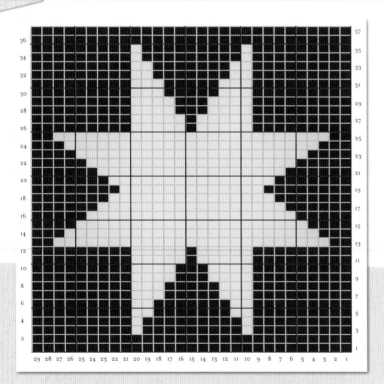

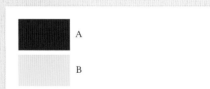

A

B

FINGERLESS LACE GLOVES

THESE LUXURIOUS FINGERLESS LACE GLOVES LOOK STUNNING and will keep you warm. Each glove is knitted in one piece, with the lace design repeating on the front and back of the long cuff, then changing to stockinette stitch for the palm of the hand. The elegant chevron finish at the end of the cuff is simply created by the lace pattern, and the thumb and hand are edged with garter stitch.

The gloves are designed to be worn up to the elbow but can easily be shortened to a more practical length by taking out one or more of the 10-row lace pattern repeats. To vamp them up for evening wear, add a row of glass beads to the bound-off edges or knit the gloves in a yarn with a metallic mix so they shimmer and sparkle.

MATERIALS:

- Debbie Bliss Andes 65% baby alpaca, 35% mulberry silk (109 yd/100 m to a 50-g skein): 3 x 50-g shade Green
- Pair each of 3.25-mm (US 3, UK 10) and 4-mm (US 6, UK 8) needles

GAUGE:

22 sts and 30 rows to 4 in (10 cm) over st st using 4-mm needles

FINISHED MEASUREMENTS:

Approx. 21 in (51 cm) length x 5½ in (14 cm) width (across palm and thumb), 4 in (10 cm) across cuff

It is a good idea to use a row counter when lace knitting, as it is easy to forget where you are in the pattern!

RIGHT GLOVE

Using 4-mm needles, cast on 58 sts.

K 2 rows.

Row 1 (RS): K3,*sl 1, k2tog, psso, k7, yfwd, k1, yrn, p1, yon, k1, yfwd, k7, k3tog**, k6, rep from * to **, k3.

Row 2 and every alt row: P14, k1, p28, k1, p14.

Row 3: K3, *sl 1, k2tog, psso, k6, (yfwd, k1) twice, p1, (k1, yfwd) twice, k6, k3tog**, k6, rep from * to **, k3.

Row 5: K3, *sl 1, k2tog, psso, k5, yfwd, k1, yfwd, k2, p1, k2, yfwd, k1, yfwd, k5, k3tog**, k6, rep from * to **, k3.

Row 7: K3, *sl 1, k2tog, psso, k4, yfwd, k1, yfwd, k3, p1, k3, yfwd, k1, yfwd, k4, k3tog**, k6, rep from * to **, k3.

Row 9: K3, *sl 1, k2tog, psso, k3, yfwd, k1, yfwd, k4, p1, k4, yfwd, k1, yfwd, k3, k3tog**, k6, rep from * to **, k3.

Row 10: P14, k1, p28, p14.

Rows 11–50: Rep rows 1–10 4 more times ***.

Row 51: K3,*sl 1, k2tog, psso, k7, yfwd, k1, yrn, p1, yon, k1, yfwd, k7, k3tog**, k4, k2tog tbl, rep from * to **, k3 (57 sts).

Row 52 and next 2 alt rows: P14, k1, p27, k1, p14.

Row 53: K3, *sl 1, k2tog, psso, k6, (yfwd, k1) twice, p1, (k1, yfwd) twice, k6, k3tog**, k5, rep from * to **, k3.

Row 55: K3, *sl 1, k2tog, psso, k5, yfwd, k1, yfwd, k2, p1, k2, yfwd, k1, yfwd, k5, k3tog**, k5, rep from * to **, k3.

Row 57: K3, *sl 1, k2tog, psso, k4, yfwd, k1, yfwd, k3, p1, k3, yfwd, k1, yfwd, k4, k3tog**, k3, k2tog tbl, rep from * to **, k3 (56 sts).

Row 58 and next 2 alt rows: P14, k1, p26, k1, p14.

Row 59: K3, *sl 1, k2tog, psso, k3, yfwd, k1, yfwd, k4, p1, k4, yfwd, k1, yfwd, k3, k3tog**, k4, rep from * to **, k3.

Row 61: K3, *sl 1, k2tog, psso, k7, yfwd, k1, yrn, p1, yon, k1, yfwd, k7, k3tog**, k4, rep from * to **, k3.

Row 63: K3, *sl 1, k2tog, psso, k6, (yfwd, k1) twice, p1, (k1, yfwd) twice, k4, k3tog**, k2, k2tog tbl, rep from * to **, k3 (55 sts).

Row 64 and next 2 alt rows: P14, k1, p25, k1, p14.

Row 65: K3, *sl 1, k2tog, psso, k5, yfwd, k1, yfwd, k2, p1, k2, yfwd, k1, yfwd, k5, k3tog**, k3, rep from * to **, k3.

Row 67: K3, *sl 1, k2tog, psso, k4, yfwd, k1, yfwd, k3, p1, k3, yfwd, k1, yfwd, k4, k3tog**, k3, rep from * to **, k3.

Row 69: K3, *sl 1, k2tog, psso, k3, yfwd, k1, yfwd, k4, p1, k4, yfwd, k1, yfwd, k3, k3tog**, k1, k2tog tbl, rep from * to **, k3 (54 sts).

Row 70 and next 2 alt rows: P14, k1, p24, k1, p14.

Row 71: K3, *sl 1, k2tog, psso, k7, yfwd, k1, yrn, p1, yon, k1, yfwd, k7, k3tog**, k2, rep from * to **, k3.

Row 73: K3, *sl 1, k2tog, psso, k6, (yfwd, k1) twice, p1, (k1, yfwd) twice, k6, k3tog**, k2, rep from * to **, k3.

Row 75: K3, *sl 1, k2tog, psso, k5, yfwd, k1, yfwd, k2, p1, k2, yfwd, k1, yfwd, k5, k3tog**, k2 tog tbl, rep from * to **, k3 (53 sts).

Row 76 and next 2 alt rows: P14, k1, p23, k1, p14.

Row 77: K3, *sl 1, k2tog, psso, k4, yfwd, k1, yfwd, k3, p1, k3, yfwd, k1, yfwd, k4, k3tog**, k1, rep from * to **, k3.

Row 79: K3, *sl 1, k2tog, psso, k3, yfwd, k1, yfwd, k4, p1, k4, yfwd, k1, yfwd, k3, k3tog**, k1, rep from * to **, k3.

SHAPE THUMB GUSSET

Row 81: K3, sl 1, k2tog, psso, k7, yfwd, k1, yrn, p1, yon, k1, yfwd, k7, k3tog, m1, k1, m1, to end (55 sts).

Rows 82 & 84: P40, k1, p14.

Row 83: K3, sl 1, k2tog, psso, k6, (yfwd, k1) twice, p1, (k1, yfwd) twice, k6, k3tog, k to end.

Row 85: K3, sl 1, k2tog, psso, k5, yfwd, k1, yfwd, k2, p1, k2, yfwd, k1, yfwd, k5, k3tog, m1, k3, m1, k to end (57 sts).

Rows 86 & 88: P42, k1, p14.

Row 87: K3, sl 1, k2tog, psso, k4, yfwd, k1, yfwd, k3, p1, k3, yfwd, k1, yfwd, k4, k3tog, to end.

Row 89: K3, sl 1, k2tog, psso, k3, yfwd, k1, yfwd, k4, p1, k4, yfwd, k1, yfwd, k3, k3tog, m1, k5, m1, to end (59 sts).

Row 90: P44, k1, p14.

Cont to inc 2 sts in this way on rows 93 and 97 and keeping patt correct work 10 rows (63 sts).

THUMB

Row 101: K3, sl 1, k2tog, psso, k7, yfwd, k1, yrn, p1, yon, k1, yfwd, k7, k3tog, k16, cast on 2 sts, turn.

Next row: P18, cast on 2 sts, turn.

Starting with a k row, cont on these 20 sts in st st for 4 rows.

Using 3.25-mm needles, work 2 rows in garter st, bind off. Sew up thumb seam.

With RS of work facing, pick up and k 2 sts from base of thumb seam, k to end of row (49 sts).

Next and foll 4 alt rows: P34, k1, p14.

Next row: K3, sl 1, k2tog, psso, k6, (yfwd, k1) twice, p1, (k1, yfwd) twice, k6, k3tog, k23.

Next RS row: K3, sl 1, k2tog, psso, k5, yfwd, k1, yfwd, k2, p1, k2, yfwd, k1, yfwd, k5, k3tog, k23.

Next RS row: K3, sl 1, k2tog, psso, k4, yfwd, k1, yfwd, k3, p1, k3, yfwd, k1, yfwd, k4, k3tog, k23.

Next RS row: K3, sl 1, k2tog, psso, k3, yfwd, k1, yfwd, k4, p1, k4, yfwd, k1, yfwd, k3, k3tog, k23.

Using 3.25-mm needles work 2 rows in garter st. Bind off.

LEFT GLOVE

Work as for right glove from beg to ***.

Row 51: K3, *sl 1, k2tog, psso, k7, yfwd, k1, yrn, p1, yon, k1, yfwd, k7, k3tog**, k2tog tbl, k4, rep from * to **, k3 (57 sts).

Rows 52–56: Same as for right glove.

Row 57: K3, *sl 1, k2tog, psso, k4, yfwd, k1, yfwd, k3, p1, k3, yfwd, k1, yfwd, k4, k3tog**, k2tog tbl, k3, rep from * to **, k3 (56 sts).

Rows 58–62: Same as for right glove.

Row 63: K3, *sl 1, k2tog, psso, k6, (yfwd, k1) twice, p1, (k1, yfwd) twice, k6, k3tog**, k2tog tbl, k2, rep from * to **, k3 (55 sts).

Rows 64–68: Same as for right glove.

Row 69: K3, *sl 1, k2tog, psso, k3, yfwd, k1, yfwd, k4, p1, k4, yfwd, k1, yfwd, k3, k3tog**, 2tog tbl, k1, rep from * to ** k3 (54 sts).

Rows 70–80: Same as for right glove.

Shape thumb gusset.

Row 81: K26, m1, k1, m1, sl 1, k2tog, psso, k7, yfwd, k1, yrn, p1, yon, k1, yfwd, k7, k3tog, k3 (55 sts).

Row 82: P14, k1, p40.

Row 83: K29, sl 1, k2tog, psso, k6, (yfwd, k1) twice, p1, (k1, yfwd) twice, k6, k3tog, k3.

Row 84: P14, k1, p40.

Row 85: K26, m1, k3, m1, sl 1, k2tog, psso, k5, yfwd, k1, yfwd, k2, p1, k2, yfwd, k1, yfwd, k5, k3tog, k3 (57 sts).

Row 86: P14, k1, p42.

Row 87: K31, sl 1, k2tog, psso, k4, yfwd, k1, yfwd, k3, p1, k3, yfwd, k1, yfwd, k4, k3tog, k3.

Row 88: P14, k1, p42.

Row 89: K26, m1, k5, m1, sl 1, k2tog, psso, k3, yfwd, k1, yfwd, k4, p1, k4, yfwd, k1, yfwd, k3,

k3tog, k3 (59 sts).

Row 90: P14, k1, p44.

Row 91: K33, sl 1, k2tog, psso, k7, yfwd, k1, yrn, p1, yon, k1, yfwd, k7, k3tog, k3.

Row 92: P14, k1, p44.

Row 93: K26, m1, k7, m1, sl 1, k2tog, psso, k6, (yfwd, k1) twice, p1, (k1, yfwd) twice, k6, k3tog, k3 (61 sts).

Row 94: P14, k1, p46.

Row 95: K35, sl 1, k2tog, psso, k5, yfwd, k1, yfwd, k2, p1, k2, yfwd, k1, yfwd, k5, k3tog, k3.

Row 96: P14, k1, p46.

Row 97: K26, m1, k9, m1, sl 1, k2tog, psso, k4, yfwd, k1, yfwd, k3, p1, k3, yfwd, k1, yfwd, k4, k3tog, k3 (63 sts).

Row 98: P14, k1, p48.

Row 99: K37, sl 1, k2tog, psso, k3, yfwd, k1, yfwd, k4, p1, k4, yfwd, k1, yfwd, k3, k3tog, k3.

Row 100: P14, k1, p48.

THUMB

Row 101: K37, cast on 2 sts, turn.

Next row: P18, cast on 2 sts, turn.

Work 4 rows in st st on these 20 sts. Change to 3.25-mm needles, work 2 rows in garter st, bind off. Sew up thumb seam.

With the RS facing, pick up and k 2 sts from base of thumb seam, sl 1, k2tog, psso, k7, yfwd, k1, yrn, p1, yon, k1, yfwd, k7, k3tog, k3 (49 sts).

Next and foll 4 alt rows: P14, k1, p34.

Next RS row: K23, sl 1, k2tog, psso, k6, (yfwd, k1) twice, p1, (k1, yfwd) twice, k6, k3tog, k3.

Next RS row: K23, sl 1, k2tog, psso, k5, yfwd, k1, yfwd, k2, p1, k2, yfwd, k1, yfwd, k5, k3tog, k3.

Next RS row: K23, sl 1, k2tog, psso, k4, yfwd, k1, yfwd, k3, p1, k3, yfwd, k1, yfwd, k4, k3tog, k3.

Next RS row: K23, sl 1, k2tog, psso, k3, yfwd, k1, yfwd, k4, p1, k4, yfwd, k1, yfwd, k3, k3tog, k3.

Using 3.25-mm needles work 2 rows in garter st. Bind off.

FINISHING UP

Pin and block with a damp cloth. Sew up the side seams and sew in any loose ends.

Wrapping a stitch on short row shaping prevents a hole from forming when you turn the knitting.

WALL CLOCK

THIS COOL, CLASSIC CLOCK FACE has 12 short cable twists to indicate the numerals, and a battery-operated timepiece. The crisp mercerized cotton gives sharp definition to the textured knitting. The inner circle is created with a simple short row shaping technique, and the outer edging is knitted in seed stitch and short cables on reversed stockinette stitch. Change the color to suit your décor: classic cream will look good against dark or patterned wall coverings; for pale walls, choose a vibrant splash of color.

Careful finishing and an even texture are important for this project. Choose a timepiece with a long spindle to make sure that the clock hands turn freely without snagging on the cotton.

MATERIALS:

- Rowan Cotton Glace 100% mercerized cotton (126 yd/115 m per 50-g ball): 2 x 50-g balls Ecru
- Small piece of waste yarn in a different shade
- Pair of 3.25-mm (US 3, UK 10) needles
- 3.25-mm circular needle (short length)
- Cable needle
- Plastic Frisbee measuring approx. 10 in (25.5 cm) in diameter
- Clock timepiece with a long spindle
- Circular piece of thin foam measuring 12 in (30 cm) in diameter
- Elastic ½ in (12 mm) width x 19½ in (50 cm) long

GAUGE:

23 sts and 32 rows to 4 in (10 cm) over st st using 3.25-mm needles

FINISHED MEASUREMENTS:

Approx 12 in (30 cm) in diameter from fold lines

SPECIAL ABBREVIATION

C6F—place 3 sts on cable needle at front of work, k3, k3 from cn.

TIP

One simple way to change the look of the clock would be to use a different color of yarn for the outside edge.

CENTER OF CLOCK FACE

Using 3.25-mm needles and waste yarn, cast on 18 sts using the thumb method.

Change to main yarn.

Row 1 (WS): P.

Rows 2–3: K12, turn, wrap 1, p to end.

Rows 4–5: K6, turn, wrap 1, p to end.

Rows 6–7: K12, turn, wrap 1, p to end.

Row 8: K18.

Rep rows 1–8 (14 times). Leave the 18 sts on the needle, place the cast-on 18 sts on a needle and neatly graft the two sets of stitches together, gently pulling out the piece of waste thread.

OUTER EDGE OF CLOCK FACE

With the RS of work facing and using the circular needle, pick up and k 120 sts around the edge of the center circle. Using a st marker to indicate the beg of each round cont as follows:

Round 1: K1, p1, to end.

Rounds 2–4: Rep round 1.

Rounds 5–6: P.

Round 7: *P10, M1, rep from * to last 10 sts, k9 inc 1 in last st (132 sts).

Round 8: *P5, k6, rep from * to end of round.

Round 9: As round 8.

Round 10: *P5, C6F, rep from * to end of round.

Rounds 11–12: As round 8.

Round 13: As round 10.

Round 14: As round 8.

Rounds 15–22: K.

Round 23: P (this forms a fold line).

Rounds 24–31: K.

Bind off.

FINISHING UP

Pin and block.

Fold outer edge of clock face at the fold line and slip stitch this hem to the back of work, leaving a small gap to insert elastic. Place a safety pin on one end of the elastic and feed this into the hem you have just made, working the elastic all the way around until it appears out of the gap. Stretch the elastic slightly so that it is taut and sew the two ends together, push back inside the hem and close the gap. Fasten off any loose ends.

Place the foam over the Frisbee and lightly glue it in place to make handling easier. Make a hole through the foam and the Frisbee exactly at the center point. This hole needs to be large enough for the spindle from the timepiece to go through.

Place the knitted piece over the foam and Frisbee and attach the timepiece. If necessary, tighten the elastic to make the knitted cover fit securely.

ABBREVIATIONS

beg—beginning

cm—centimeter

cn—cable needle

cont—continue

dec—decrease

dpn—double-pointed needle

ft—feet

g—gram

g-st—garter stitch

in—inch

inc—increase

k—knit

k2tog—knit 2 together

LH—left-hand

m—meter

m1—make 1 by picking up the bar in front of the next st to be worked and knitting into it

mm—millimeter

p—purl

patt—pattern

psso—pass slip stitch over

rep—repeat

RH—right-hand

RS—right side

skpo—slip 1, knit 1, pass slip stitch over

sl—slip

st(s)—stitch(es)

st st—stockinette stitch

tbl—through back of loop

tog—together

wrap 1—with yarn at back, slip stitch on right-hand needle to left needle, bring yarn to front and slip stitch back onto right-hand needle

WS—wrong side

yfwd—yarn forward

yon—yarn over needle

yrn—yarn round needle

NEEDLE CONVERSION CHART

Knitting needle conversion

Metric size (mm)	US size	UK size
2	0	14
2.25	1	13
2.5	-	-
2.75	2	12
3	-	11
3.25	3	10
3.5	4	-
3.75	5	9
4	6	8
4.5	7	7
5	8	6
5.5	9	5
6	10	4
6.5	10½	3
7	-	2
7.5	-	1
8	11	0
9	13	00
10	15	000
12	17	-
16	19	-
19	35	-
25	50	-

Crochet hook conversion

Metric size (mm)	US size
2.25	B1
2.5	-
2.75	C2
3	-
3.25	D3
3.5	E4
3.75	F5
4	G6
4.5	7
5	H8
5.5	I9
6	J10
6.5	K101/2
8	L11
9	M/N13
10	N/P15
12	O16

INDEX

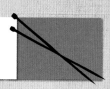